Out of the Darkness

Out of the Darkness

Tina Nash

SIMON &
SCHUSTER

London · New York · Sydney · Toronto · New Delhi

A CBS COMPANY

First published in Great Britain by Simon & Schuster UK Ltd, 2012
A CBS company

This book is a work of non-fiction based on the life, experiences and recollections of the author. In some limited cases names of people, places, dates, sequences or the detail of events have been changed solely to protect the privacy of others. The author has stated to the publishers that, except in such minor respects not affecting the substantial accuracy of the work, the contents of this book are true.

The right of Tina Nash to be identified as the author of this work has been asserted by her in accordance with sections 77 and 78 of the Copyright, Designs and Patents Act, 1988.

1 3 5 7 9 10 8 6 4 2

Simon & Schuster UK Ltd
1st Floor
222 Gray's Inn Road
London WC1X 8HB

www.simonandschuster.co.uk

Simon & Schuster Australia,
Sydney

Simon & Schuster India,
New Delhi

A CIP catalogue record for this book is available from the British Library

ISBN: 978-1-47111-466-3
ISBN: 978-1-47111-467-0 (ebook)

Typeset by Hewer Text UK Ltd, Edinburgh
Printed in the UK by CPI Group (UK) Ltd, Croydon, CR0 4YY

To my sons, Ben and Liam

Contents

I

Fresh Start

They say you should never move back to where you grew up. I should have listened.

I zigzagged my way through the sand dunes to Hayle Beach where I hadn't set foot in twelve years since I left home at seventeen. Nothing had changed in the sleepy Cornish village and, with every footstep, another childhood memory rushed through me.

'Oi, Ben, don't go in too deep,' I yelled at my eldest son as he plunged into the sea.

I had changed though. I had come back to town with two sons by different dads and a series of dead-end relationships behind me. Some of my happiest times had been playing with my brothers and sisters in Hayle so, when a housing association property came free on the same estate where Mum raised us, I jumped at the chance to start a fresh life.

I lifted my two-year-old, Liam, into my arms and hugged him against my hip as I sauntered across the three-mile golden beach to keep a closer eye on where Ben was splashing around. It was a hot August day in 2009. The sand scorched my bare feet but there's nothing like that feeling between your toes to remind you of happy holidays. I craned my neck to the sun and basked in the heat for a moment like a seal on a rock. Life wasn't that bad after all.

'Mum, look at this!' Twelve-year-old Ben held out his hand proudly. It was a pink starfish that looked like someone had taken big bites out of it.

'Well done, Ben,' I said, ruffling my hand through his black hair. His whole freckly face lit up. I may have had Ben when I was very young but my kids meant the world to me and not for one second did I regret becoming a mum at sixteen.

My choice in men, however, left a lot to be desired. I'd been with Liam's father, a chef called Paul, for four years, but that hadn't worked out, and my last boyfriend of a year had left me emotionally drained, as he'd disappear for days on end and then turn up half a dozen times at my house on the same day craving my attention. I never knew where I stood with him and I'd had enough.

I stamped my foot in the sea, splashing water up Ben's legs.

'Oi, Mum,' Ben whined, but smiling at the thought of a water fight. He thumped his big foot forward, sending a tidal wave of salty sea up my leg and arm. Liam screeched with delight.

'Cheeky,' I yelped, holding Liam close as I started chasing after Ben.

'No, Mum,' he squealed, sprinting off down the beach.

There were lots of people on the beach that day with their towels and windbreaks and kites. One little boy had built a massive sandcastle right by the sea, so the moat whooshed full of water every time the waves came in. I smiled, as it reminded me of the fun I used to get up to with my sisters and brother Paul.

We used to be proper naughty. We'd go 'clothes-pegging' at the caravan parks – taking washing from the lines. I remembered screaming my head off while being chased across the park by an angry holidaymaker. I felt guilty now, but I was young and would do anything for a bit of excitement. Snatching milk bottles from doorsteps was another favourite pastime. We'd build dens in abandoned sheds or in the woods by the railway station and then round up twenty milk bottles and spend the day drinking them. It wasn't all random thieving though. There was the time I found a stray Labrador on our camp – Mum went mad when I brought it home with us.

'What the hell is that?' she screamed on our doorstep as I fed my new friend biscuits.

'Please, Mum,' I begged, my blonde tomboy hair falling in front of my eyes.

'No. Get rid of it,' she yelled, slamming the door.

Mum was very strict and would often lose her rag but it wouldn't stop us having fun. We didn't have a lot growing up but we made the most of what we had and it taught me to be a survivor. Having family and friends you can count on is all you need to get through life. That was why I decided to come back to Hayle – most of my family were still within a stone's throw.

'Ben,' I yelled up the beach. 'We're going to Nan's now,' I ordered, directing him up the sand dunes with my finger.

My nan still lived in the same house as when I'd left Hayle, a two-minute stroll from the beach past the tiny police station on the left. I could smell warm baked cake as I walked up the drive.

'Hello, love.' She greeted me with a smile and a big bear hug.

Nan was like a mother to me. In fact, I was much closer to her than my mum, who never seemed to have time for us. Walking into her lounge was like stepping back in time. I was now twenty-nine but everything was exactly the same as when I was five years old, when I used to jump around on her brown and white carpet pretending I was a horse. She still had the floor-length cream curtains with mocha swirly flowers, and the 1970s fake-wood electric heater built into a stone-paved wall which resembled the markings of a giraffe.

'Cup of tea and cake, love?'

'Oh, go on then, Nan,' I teased. She always baked for me and the kids, and I had a strong feeling she'd made my favourite.

'Coconut cake, you shouldn't have,' I giggled, as she brought out a slice on her faded crockery and placed it before me on her blue-checked tablecloth. The sound of her pouring tea from the pot was warm and comforting. I always felt safe and loved around Nan and it was like time stood still with her, as she never seemed to age. She was wearing her usual ankle-length skirt, tights with flat blue brogues and a blouse with buttons done up to her neck. 'Queenie' we used to call her, as she looked just like Her Majesty when she stepped out of the salon with her set and blow dry.

'So, when's the wedding?' Nan asked with a cheeky grin.

'I've had enough of men,' I sighed, hugging my cup of tea with both hands.

'What about that lad you've been dating for the past year?' she asked, breaking off a piece of cake.

I took a deep breath, shocked at the nerve she'd touched. 'He's not making me happy,' I said in a small, quiet voice. I could feel tears prickling at the back of my eyes. I wasn't going to tell Nan how Sam's erratic behaviour of being nice one minute and cold the next had left me feeling lonely and insecure. A tear trickled down my cheek.

'Stop being silly, sort yourself out,' Nan said, just like she used to when we cried as kids.

'Where's the Tina gone who used to get back on that horse when she fell off?' she joked. I spent my teenage years riding giant show horses for a trainer. I'd fall off into prickly gorse bushes, cut my arms and legs open, but I always got back in the saddle. I was fearless back then.

'I won't be seeing any of those tears. Have another piece of cake.' She smiled, cutting another sliver. She was right. I couldn't let another break-up take over. I breathed in deeply through my nose and nodded at Nan, as if to say I was listening to her. I'd seen my mum go through hundreds of break-ups and be treated badly by men and I wasn't going to stand for that. I prided myself on being a no-nonsense girl who didn't take any rubbish from blokes and I wasn't about to start now.

My two-bed semi-detached house was on the next street up from Nan's. It wasn't a patch on my place in St Ives, but I needed a new beginning. Later that Saturday night, as I was sitting alone watching a soppy romcom, it was harder to convince myself I'd made the right move. The boys were with Liam's dad, and all I had for company was the dirty smudges left on the walls by the previous tenant.

This place is a dump, I thought, scanning the poorly fitted wooden floorboards with gaps big enough to trip you up. I'd always been incredibly house-proud and the mess was bringing me down and making me feel even more lonely.

Stop being an idiot, Tina, I told myself. I was just reaching for the packet of biscuits when I heard a rap at my door. I craned my neck around, almost expecting someone else to answer it.

Bang-bang-bang! Whoever it was they were persistent.

It was my sister Lorraine.

'C'mon, we're going out,' she said, charging into my living room dressed in her clubbing gear.

'But look at the state of me,' I said, pointing at my hooded jumper and tracksuit bottoms.

'We're going to Mandy's birthday in Penzance. Get in the shower,' she ordered.

Lorraine was almost as stubborn as I was. She had long dark-brown hair and looked the spitting image of our mum before she went bottle-blonde. She was a year younger than me and loved her partying and she conveniently lived just outside Penzance, not far from me.

I was a natural blonde when I was a teenager but I'd hit the bleach over the last ten years and got myself a nickname, Pamela Nash, for looking a little like Pamela Anderson from the TV series *Baywatch*, and because I loved the beach life. Lorraine pulled out the straighteners and started ironing my long white locks while I got to work plying my eyes with glittery green shadow. Applying eye make-up was one of my favourite rituals in my going-out routine, and I always spent ages making them look bright and sparkling to bring out my baby blues.

'What about this?' I asked, holding up a black dress. Although I was tiny at five-foot-four and weighed only eight and a half stone, I didn't like to show off my slim figure. Mum had drilled it into us as kids that we had to dress conservatively – although it was a different story for her.

'You're not going out dressed like that,' she'd bark when I came down the stairs wearing a simple vest top. 'Get back upstairs,' she spat. Her voice still resonated in my head and had left a big dent in my confidence.

'Yeah, wear that with your sparkling heels,' Lorraine encouraged.

'Nah,' I said, suddenly feeling self-conscious, recoiling back into my bedroom. I reappeared wearing black trousers, a white vest top and a short black sequinned waistcoat. I did a twirl, although I wasn't feeling in the mood at all that night.

'You'll be getting all the boys looking at you,' Lorraine said, then pushed me out the door.

The birthday party involved dinner at a medieval meadery in Penzance. I'd had a few glasses of wine by the time the bill came and agreed we should go on to a club and let our hair down. Penzance is a small place – a couple of mini-supermarkets and clothes and jewellery shops on a hilly high street minutes from the promenade, which is lined with a row of restaurants and bed and breakfasts. It's the very last stop on the UK's railway into the South West – literally the end of the line. It's the kind of town where everyone knows everyone's business and I recognised the same faces even after years away.

'Watch out, the Nashers are out tonight,' the bouncer guarding the door at the Barn nightclub joked.

'Your sister Tracey not with you?' he went on.

It was like being back at school. There were six of us so our nicknames still stuck after all those years.

'Trace is married now with kids. She can't go out clubbing. Now let us in, you bugger,' I joked, teetering through into the town's only decent club.

'Shots?' Lorraine said, heading for the bar.

I linked my arm through hers and let her lead the way. It had been so long since I'd had fun I'd almost forgotten what it was like to put aside my worries for a night. I watched as the barman lined up our miniature glasses and poured them full of tequila from a great height, splashing the remainder across the bar. We licked our wrists, doused them with salt, clinked glasses and knocked back our shots.

'Eugh,' I grimaced at the bitter burn in my mouth.

'Suck on this,' Lorraine said, handing me a slice of lemon to finish it off. She then grabbed my hand and led us to the dance floor. Dancing and horse riding had been my two passions growing up and it was where I felt most confident. I threw my hands into the air to catch the strobe lighting and curved my hips from side to side.

I could feel someone's eyes watching me.

I twirled, punching the air to the music that was so loud I could feel it thump through me.

I could feel someone's eyes boring into me.

I twizzled around and our eyes locked. He was gorgeous. Dark shaved hair, chiselled jaw, muscles popping out of his fitted blue-checked shirt and mysterious dark eyes. He looked like a rugby player at six-foot-four and weighing at least eighteen stone. He rested his elbow on the bar like he knew he was a looker. He was like a magnet pulling me in. I tottered over with my drunken courage and threw my hands onto my hips.

'Do you remember me?' I asked.

Ten years earlier – August 1999

'Da, da, da . . .' I bounced on the spot clutching my big head-phones with both hands. I pushed a dial on my decks to increase the bass. I'd just spent £2,000 on my new DJ kit with the dream of becoming a professional touring the clubs. I always had at least one dream playing around in my head, something to hope for; I was that kind of girl.

I was changing tracks when my doorbell gonged.

'Just a minute!' I shouted. I teased my fingers through my curly blonde hair to give it some volume. I looked like a surfer girl with tanned skin and sea-bleached hair, wearing a simple vest and skirt and flip-flops. I could smell the waves from my flat in Newlyn, the next town along the coast from Penzance.

'All right, Tina,' said my friend Granite. Everyone had nick-names and he was no exception.

'This is Shane Jenkin,' he said, pointing to a guy who was hovering in the shadows behind him.

My cheeks burned red with embarrassment. I'd seen Shane around town and instantly had a crush on him. He was big, athletic, with dark chocolate-coloured eyes that you wanted to dive into. He looked American, wearing a Chicago Bulls shiny red and white cropped jacket. I waited to hear his accent.

'Hi,' he said. There was nothing distinct about his voice other than a slight Cornish twang.

'Come in, I was just messing around on my decks,' I said, standing back and letting the lads pass into my living room. Shane sat next to me and I could feel the sexual tension burning a hole in the space between us. We talked for hours about music and our mutual love of rapper 2Pac. He was charming and fun and I didn't want him to leave, we were getting on so well. My best friend Danielle, a hairdresser, turned up at my door a bit later that evening to join in the fun.

'Come here,' she beckoned from the kitchen, trying to keep her voice down so as not to be heard.

I flashed her a look to say 'leave me be' but she was very persistent.

'Psssst, come 'ere,' she went on, pulling a face behind Shane's back. I reluctantly peeled myself away and crept in to hear what was so important. She grabbed my arm and pulled me towards her.

'What the hell is he doing here?' she said, pointing to Shane. 'He's a bloody psycho,' she shrieked, scraping her curly hair back with her hands.

'Shhhhhh,' I cringed, not wanting him to hear. 'What are you on about?' I asked, shaking my head with confusion.

'He's just got out of prison for stamping on a guy's head and giving him brain damage.'

'What?' I choked.

'Four and a half years he's been inside,' she said, looping her finger around to imitate a crazy person. I clutched my elbows tightly into my side like I always did when I was scared. My eyes were now wide like saucers as I saw Shane get up and approach the kitchen.

'What are you girls gossiping about?' Shane said. His broad muscly chest was puffed out like a rooster. You could smell the testosterone seeping off him.

'Nothing.' Danni cut him dead, walking off into the next room.

'Don't leave me, Danni,' I whispered, pulling a face of terror.

Shane knew something was up, that's why he was trying to get me on my own. Pick me off from the group. I pressed my lips together nervously to fake a smile. He bulldozed forward, locking me into the corner, towering over my tiny frame. I was pressed up against the counter with nowhere to escape. I clutched on to the work surface behind me as he stared into me with his intense eyes.

'What?' I mouthed.

He pressed against me and leaned forward for a kiss.

'No,' I snapped, dodging his mouth. I heaved him away. I could feel his well-defined muscles under my fingers; he was built like a tank.

'Eeek, scary,' I mouthed to Danni, as I rushed to join her in the lounge. I kept my distance from Shane the rest of the evening and he eventually left with Granite a couple of hours later.

'How dare he force himself on me like that,' I said, lifting my arms in the air with anger.

'Stay away from him,' Danni warned. 'He's trouble.'

August 2009

Those words of warning I could barely hear in my head for all the alcohol Lorraine and I had knocked back that night.

'Do you remember me?' I asked Shane. He was now thirty but he hadn't changed much over ten years, he was just even better-looking and twice as big.

He looked at me intensely and then blinked.

'Yes,' he grunted. Lorraine and I chatted to him and his friend for a while and I kept catching Shane's eyes watching me.

'I don't want to go home yet, let's find a party,' moaned Lorraine, as the DJ announced the final song.

'Party?' Shane interrupted. 'I know a party, back at my place,' he laughed. He had a childish way about him which was endearing. We hailed a taxi and the four of us clambered in stinking of alcohol and sweat from dancing all night. I sat next to Shane and was pushed on top of him, he was so big. I could feel his warmth penetrating me and it reminded me of that cosy feeling that comes with having a boyfriend. I felt a pang of sadness for the car-crash relationship I'd just escaped from. I suddenly got on the defence and fired Shane a load of questions to see if he made the grade or was just like all the others.

'Have you got a job?' I asked, grabbing the headrest as we turned a corner.

'I'm a painter and decorator,' he said, his chest puffing out with pride.

'Oh, right. Do you have your own place?' I asked.

'Yes I do,' he laughed.

'Oh, right. Do you have a girlfriend?' I badgered.

'Is this the Spanish Inquisition?' he chortled, throwing his head back.

'Yeah, give him a break,' Lorraine teased on the other side of me.

But I didn't want to give him a break. I was fed up of giving men the benefit of the doubt.

'Nope,' he smiled, looking me in the eyes. 'And before you ask, I've been single for seven months.'

A butterfly fluttered its wings in my stomach when he said that and I realised I liked him.

'Oh, right,' I flirted back. Shane's place was very close to the centre of town, a ground-floor flat. It looked barely lived in, with no pictures on the walls or ornaments in it, but it was clean and tidy. Every room was painted white, in keeping with the fresh seaside feel of the town. He threw himself onto the sofa while I nestled into the chair beside him. He opened up some cans of beer and I opened up my heart. The stress and upset of the past six months came pouring out of me and he just sat and listened. By the end of the evening I was sitting next to him on the sofa while he lay stretched out behind me.

'I've said too much,' I blushed, crossing my arms defensively.

'It's all right,' he said, rubbing my back sympathetically. He seemed caring and loving, a far cry from the forceful Shane that had me pinned against the kitchen counter ten years earlier. I smiled at him and fell into his dark eyes. I wanted to kiss him there and then but I pulled my urge away. I wasn't ready to let someone in just yet – although I could already tell there was something different about Shane from all the others.

It was 6 a.m. by the time Lorraine and I decided to call it a night. I felt emotionally exhausted but also like a weight had been lifted off my shoulders, thanks to Shane listening. It was light outside and the birds were cheeping as we said goodbye on his doorstep.

'I want to see you again,' he insisted. 'Can I have your number?'

I didn't hesitate for a second. I felt like I could trust him; that he was caring and loving and, if nothing else came of it, he would make a good friend. He leaned forward and gave me a hug. He didn't try to kiss me or touch me, he was the perfect gentleman. The taxi beeped and Lorraine grabbed my arm to go.

'You've got yourself a real catch there,' Lorraine said as we drove off.

2

Falling in Love

'Call him up now,' Shane ordered Lorraine to dial my ex-boyfriend from her mobile.

'No,' I cringed, cowering in the corner of Shane's lounge. We'd been dating for a couple of weeks and I'd let it slip that my ex had been hounding me, trying to get us back together. All girls know there is nothing like sparking a bit of jealousy in a man to see if he's really interested in you.

'Hold on a minute,' Lorraine giggled, scrolling through her phone. It all seemed a bit of a game at first, thanks to a few glasses of wine and cans of cider, but Shane was getting worked up.

'No, please stop, Lorraine.' I didn't think she was going to go through with it.

'It's ringing,' she squealed, holding the phone up high out of my reach.

'Oh, God, noooo.' I ran into the hallway out of embarrassment. I held my hands over my ears like a kid watching a scary film. It didn't stop me hearing Shane's booming voice barking orders down the phone.

'Stop ringing Tina. She's with me now, we're together,' he told my ex.

My legs buckled, but more out of excitement than embarrassment. I'd never had a man fight for me like that. A smile spread across my face as I realised I was his, we were together – he wanted me.

I'd see Shane on Tuesday and Saturday nights when my kids stayed over at Liam's dad Paul's house. We'd text and speak on the phone regularly but he didn't crowd me, he didn't put pressure on me, which suited me perfectly because I was still struggling to get over a break-up. I wasn't bowled over by Shane at first, if I was honest; he was more of a port in a storm, but he quickly grew on me. They say it's the relationships that catch you off guard that end up getting under your skin.

When I was around his flat I felt like I was on holiday from my life of being a mum-of-two. He took me away from my worries and gave me back my youth. We'd been together for three weeks when I took the plunge and invited him back to mine – into my world. I was nervous about Shane meeting my kids though. What if he suddenly realised he didn't want a mum for a girlfriend? He was so good-looking why would he want to be with me? Those fears were quickly washed away with the tide when he caught the train to Hayle from Penzance. I got my neighbour Zara to baby-sit while I went to meet Shane at the station down the road.

I felt like a teenager on a first date as I waited on the platform. It was a balmy summer evening but I was shivering from nerves and buried my mouth into the neck of my hooded jumper to keep warm. It was a good thing I was hiding my face, as my jaw dropped when I saw Shane jump off the train. His chest was so big his XL T-shirt clung to him like cellophane, highlighting his pectoral muscles. His blue jeans moulded to his thighs, showing off his pert bum. I'd never fancied anyone so much in my life. He swaggered over but then stopped dead in front of me.

'All right?' I asked, beaming from ear to ear that he had travelled to see me.

He looked at me with big puppy-dog eyes and blinked. His arms remained limply by his side like he didn't know what to do with himself. I stood on my tiptoes and planted a kiss on his lips.

'Come on, then.' I grabbed his hand. Shane acted like he'd never been loved before, like he didn't know what to do if someone hugged or kissed him or showed him affection. It immediately tugged on my heartstrings and made me want to mother him.

'Here we are,' I said, nervously turning the key in my front door. What's he going to think of me when he sees my place? I thought in a panic.

'Nice place,' he said, confidently striding into the lounge where Zara was looking after the boys.

'Hello, mate,' he said, patting Liam's head. I didn't get it – one minute he was shy, the next he was bold as brass. But he seemed to have a way with kids, which melted my heart even more.

'What you playing on the Xbox, mate?' he asked Ben, who was sitting cross-legged on the floor playing computer games.

'Errr football, Pro Evolution,' Ben replied shyly.

Shane strode over and sat down next to him, bending his big legs like a giant pretzel.

'Two player?' He asked to join in. Ben handed him a spare controller and the pair of them started battling it out on the pitch. My kid versus the big kid, it appeared. I thanked Zara for baby-sitting and saw her off at the door. She stuck both thumbs up, grinning enthusiastically, as if to say I was on to a winner with Shane.

'Stop it,' I joked, ushering her out, but another butterfly flapped its wings in my stomach as someone else was telling me what a catch Shane was.

Once the boys had been put to bed we spent the evening watching DVDs and chatting. It was like he'd caught verbal diarrhoea all of a sudden – he even paused the films so he could talk to me more. Shane told me how he used to be a professional rugby player on the Cornish Pirates reserves team, and he originally wanted to become a Marine just like his old man. He admitted he did go to prison ten years ago for beating a guy up, but said he didn't do it; he had taken the rap for his friend. He assured me he had turned his life around.

'I can't stand people using violence to get what they want,' he stated, as he told a story about some of the friends he used to hang around with.

'It's not right, you know, to go around beating the shit out of people,' he said righteously.

I sat next to him on the sofa, mesmerised by this giant who was actually a big teddy bear. He was so huge I almost slipped underneath him as we cuddled and kissed. He took my arm and gently stroked it like he was handling a precious porcelain doll.

He was supposed to get up early for work the next day but we spent the whole morning making love.

'How do you not crush me?' I giggled as he rolled back on top of me.

'Because I spread my weight evenly.' He rolled his eyes child-ishly. He gently nibbled at my neck and then laid a trail of kisses to my ear and then back to my mouth. His tongue was soft and tender and I felt an explosion in my stomach that spread like fire across my body, all the way from my fingers, which he grasped passionately in his hands, to down below. He was slow and gentle as he moved in and out of me and I fell deep into his dark eyes that were dilating with every thrust. I never expected such a big hulk of a man to be so gentle in bed. I fell asleep wrapped in his bear hug. Sweaty, exhausted, but happy.

My internal alarm clock to wake up and check on little Liam again was ringing. I rolled over to give Shane a kiss but I stopped in my tracks to just enjoy the moment. I watched as he lay there on his back, fast asleep, his big chest heaving up and down with every breath. The morning sun poured through my curtains, shining over his muscly body, highlighting the tattoos across his chest and arms. I hadn't really taken a close look at them until now. Is that what I think it is? I peered closer, trying to be quiet so as not to wake him. Down his right arm was an image of a hooded executioner raising his sword like he was about to slaughter someone.

Eugh.

But there was more. On his left chest was a tattoo of a tiger ripping someone's head off. Down his left arm was OUTLAW in big bold black letters. I chuckled at the thought that Shane fancied himself as a bit of an outlaw. Why would he want to have such nasty violent tattoos covering his body? Maybe he got them when he was much younger? I brushed off my concerns by thinking that they were just something to do with his hard-man image.

It was late afternoon by the time Shane surfaced from my bedroom. He plodded down the stairs rubbing his bleary eyes while I was busy preparing tea for the boys.

'Evening,' I joked.

He came up behind me and pulled me into him; his warmth covered my back like a blanket and I melted. He was just about to turn me around and kiss me when his phone vibrated.

'Oh shit, it's my boss,' he said, taking the call into the next room. Shane told me he had finished the painting job he was working on, so what was he worried about? I craned my neck to listen in but the conversation was over in seconds. Shane stood there looking bemused.

'What?' I asked, worried.

'He said I'm fired because I was supposed to be working today. I was meant to redo the gloss I'd painted.'

'No.' I clasped my face in my hands.

'He's just being a prick,' Shane said calmly.

'I feel really bad because you spent the day with me,' I said.

'He'll get over it. He needs me,' Shane boasted.

He sounded like he had it under control, so I dropped the subject, but I'd given myself a bit of a shock – I must like Shane if I was starting to feel responsible for him. He was supposed to be a rebound. A time-filler. I got angry with myself for letting my guard slip.

'Are you going home tonight, then?' I asked Shane, as he picked at food in my fridge. My defences were back up.

'Let's watch another DVD,' he suggested. One look at his puppy-dog face and I caved in once more. I knew I'd be strong again by the time the weekend came around.

But the butterflies returned, and the loving feeling burned even stronger the next time I saw him. He was such a natural with my kids and they seemed to adore him too. He whisked Ben away for a bike ride along the country lanes while I stayed at home preparing a lavish meal. I'd always loved cooking but I hadn't bothered so much in recent years. Shane had inspired me to put my chef's hat back on again, and I dug out my case of chef's knives and my old Spanish chicken recipe, which always used to get lots of compliments. Slowly but steadily I could feel myself opening up and becoming the fun, carefree Tina I used to know.

I was chopping the carrots when I found myself drifting into a daydream about Shane, or more accurately, about his body. I let out a snigger – I couldn't believe I was fantasising about sex while cutting the vegetables. Well, they do look a bit phallic! I thought, laughing to myself again. It was very rare that I really fancied someone and the chemistry between Shane and me was surprisingly explosive. I couldn't get enough of him, and I clearly couldn't stop myself thinking about him.

Shane and Ben returned muddy and sweaty but bursting with excitement.

'No dirty shoes in here,' I yelled, as they charged through the door.

'We've just seen the cutest miniature horses and pigs,' Shane gushed.

'Yeah, Mum, they are so tiny,' Ben added, his cheeks rosy from the cycle ride.

'Where? What you talking about?' I asked, trying to calm them down.

'Up at the quarry, we have to go and bring them something to eat, we have to go now,' Shane said.

I felt like saying 'calm down', as I would to my kids, because he was so excited, but it was too endearing to watch. He was grinning and bouncing around on the spot and he wouldn't stop talking about the mini-animals all night, until I eventually agreed to go and see them the following day.

Ben cycled on ahead while Shane walked his bike next to me, as we snaked our way along the country lanes towards the sand quarry. It couldn't have been a more perfect day; the sun was baking down on us and the birds were jumping between the hedgerows that lined the road. That's what I love about Cornwall, you can sometimes walk for miles without seeing a car if you know your way around the back routes.

We broke off from the lane into the sand dunes and I dug deep to start the climb. Shane watched me protectively to make sure I didn't lose my footing. The seagulls circled above, screeching as we closed in on the quarry, which looked like a giant sandpit.

'Look, Mum,' Ben shouted, pointing to the little farm animals in the adjacent field.

'Awww, they're so cute,' I squealed.

Shane opened the carrier bag and handed Ben some apples and carrots to feed the horses. Shane coaxed the horse to come forward and gently stroked its nose and mane and looked lost in a world of happiness. He seemed a natural with children and animals. I beamed. Corny as it might sound, every day I was seeing more signs that I'd finally met someone who could be the 'one'.

I was witnessing a different side to him from what everyone else saw, which made me feel special and needed. Around town everyone was afraid of Shane because he was so big and it was well known he'd done time in prison. I felt like I was next to a celebrity when we walked the streets of Penzance. Everyone would say 'All right, Shane' with their heads bowed, afraid to look him in the eye. But to me, he was like a big cuddly teddy bear who I'd managed to tame. I felt safe with him – he was like my bodyguard.

I think I was subconsciously looking for a man who would protect me, as the memories of my mum being beaten up by boyfriends had never really gone away. I couldn't believe it when Shane said he hated men who hit women – it was like he'd read my mind. He even proved it to me one night while we were staying at his place.

We were lounging around on his sofa chatting when we heard some banging noises coming from the flat above. I looked up at Shane, who clenched his jaw with irritation like he knew what was going on. The thumping and banging continued, and my heart stopped as the penny dropped. I'd heard those sorts of noises before too. Then came the crying and screaming on cue.

'No, no, no, stop it,' a woman screamed.

'WHACK!'

'Please, God, no,' she sobbed.

'SMACK!'

I shut my eyes. I was back in the caravan when I was six years old, huddling into my brother and sisters for fear of my life. I could see Mum being smacked in the face by her boyfriend like it was happening in front of me now. Smack, whack, smashing into her beautiful chiselled cheekbones. 'Come here, bitch,' he snarled, grabbing a fistful of her hair and dragging her back by her heels into the bedroom. The door slammed shut and all we could hear was screams and cries and her begging him to stop.

'WHACK!' The noise jolted me back into reality. Shane jumped up from the sofa and started pacing the room.

'What a prick, what a prick,' he shouted, flexing his muscles and rolling his shoulders back like the Incredible Hulk. He was snorting through his nose like a mad bull in a ring.

'No, please stop!' the woman screamed again.

'That's it,' he yelled, and charged up the stairs with me close on his heels.

'Shane, stop, please, don't get involved,' I begged from the corridor, but it was too late. Shane was already hammering down his neighbour's door with his fist.

'Open up,' he yelled. A stream of red anger had spread from his neck to his face and he looked like he was about to explode.

The door opened.

'What?' said a tall guy wearing a vest with greasy dark hair and sweat leaking from his forehead.

He's in for it now, I thought, as I cowered in the hall. I thought Shane was going to knock him out with the steam that was coming off him.

'I'm fed up of hearing this shit all the time. You don't fucking hit a woman,' he yelled in the guy's face.

'YOU DON'T FUCKING HIT WOMEN!' he said again, pointing his finger like a gun.

Those words were like music to my ears. I'd finally found the missing puzzle piece I'd been searching for my whole life. I swore I'd never end up with a wife-beater like my mum had, and it looked like I'd just hit the jackpot.

3

Love Games

'I thought the honeymoon period was supposed to last six months not three,' I said, slumping my head into my hands.

'He'll turn up in a minute,' my sister Lorraine tried to reassure me.

A night out on the town was a rare thing for me these days, and I'd been looking forward to dressing up and dancing with Shane. He was supposed to meet me at Lorraine's hours ago and he wasn't picking up his phone. I had a terrible sinking feeling in my gut that something wasn't right. I'd always had a strong intuition and my accuracy scared me now. Why do you care so much, Tina? Snap out of it, I chastised myself. But I couldn't. I'd fallen in love.

'You stay and finish getting ready and I'll pop down to his house,' Lorraine said, trying to help.

'Thanks, girl,' I said with a smile. It was my pet name for all my sisters.

I tried to keep myself busy straightening my hair and putting on my make-up, but that anxious feeling was gnawing inside. It was because Shane had been totally reliable up until now. He'd been the perfect gentleman – the perfect boyfriend. I couldn't understand why he had stood me up.

I jumped at the bang of the door slamming behind Lorraine. I tried to appear relaxed but my sister knew me all too well.

'What?' Something was wrong. It was written all over her face.

She took a deep breath and then reluctantly broke the news.

'The reason he's not picking up is because he's busy entertaining a flat full of girls,' she said, raising her eyebrows.

My heart sank into my stomach. 'What do you mean, he's with girls?' I stammered.

'He's getting drunk with a flat full of all these young women,' she explained again.

My knees buckled, as a thousand jealous thoughts raced through my mind. I imagined him cuddling up to all these young beautiful blondes. I sat on the sofa and scraped my hands through my hair.

'Oh my God, I'm such an idiot. I thought he liked me,' I said, looking up to Lorraine for confirmation.

She bit her lip, unsure of what to say. We'd always been there for each other's heartbreaks and she could tell I was in pain.

'He *does* like . . .' she started when her mobile ring interrupted.

'It's Shane,' she said, looking at the flashing number.

I was angry. I'd been waiting for him all night and he'd stood me up to party with a load of girls. I wasn't standing for that. I had more self-respect than that.

'He wants to speak to you,' Lorraine said, holding the phone out to me.

'No,' I snapped. 'I don't want to speak to him, thanks.'

Lorraine relayed the message tentatively and then looked to me for further instructions.

'Come on, we're still going out.' I winked at her. I wasn't letting any guy get the better of me, no matter how much it hurt inside. I quickly threw on some black tailored trousers and a blue boob tube with white hearts and doused myself in one of Lorraine's perfumes.

'We're off,' I announced. But just as I opened the front door Shane turned up in a taxi. His eyes were red and droopy like he'd been drinking for hours. He flashed me a sheepish grin and opened his arms wide to give me a bear hug.

'No,' I said, pushing him away. 'Who were those girls you were with?' I demanded. I wasn't going to beat around the bush. I didn't share my boyfriends with other girls.

'No, no, it's nothing like that,' he pleaded, moving in to give me a kiss.

'Really?' I held my arm out to keep him away.

'They're just friends,' he said, trying to win back my trust. 'Friends I've known for ages.' He trailed off impatiently.

I stared hard at him for a few moments but my armour was pierced as soon as he flashed me his winning smile. Maybe these girls *were* just friends of his? He'd had a life before me. And he came across as so sincere.

'OK,' I mumbled, and he pulled me into his arms. But as we cuddled, that anxious feeling returned. I had it in my head that he was more of a catch than I was. That as a mum of two I couldn't compete with those young girls he was flirting with. Maybe he'd got bored with me, that's why he was out meeting new girls? I'd never doubted myself like this in any relationship before, so why was I doing so now? Things weren't quite right but I couldn't put my finger on it.

I put aside my worries for the time being and we all clambered in the taxi and headed to the local nightclub. Lorraine and I had some catching up to do, as Shane had already sunk a few ciders and was more boisterous than I'd seen him before. Lorraine rolled her eyes as if to say 'boys will be boys' and we tottered in our heels to the bar to knock back our favourite shots while Shane said hello to half the club, who all knew his face.

We were making some shapes on the dance floor when Lorraine grabbed my arm and spun me around.

'What's Shane doing?' she gasped.

I watched in horror as he yanked his belt out of his jeans and tugged it taut between both hands like a garrotte.

Shane rolled his shoulders back and flexed his muscles like he was an ape. All he needed to do was beat his chest and he would be King of the Jungle. I didn't have a clue what he was about to do.

'Want some of this?' he snarled, thrusting his belt in the face of a stranger walking past the bar.

'Oh my God,' I gasped, covering my mouth in disbelief. The guy looked at him like he was nuts and carried on walking.

'Come on, then.' Shane pushed into his back.

He was starting a fight with a random guy. 'What an idiot,' I said to Lorraine. 'Come on, I'm going home.' I signalled towards the cloakroom. Shane was quick off the mark and reached his long arm out to stop me. I shrugged him off but he spun me around.

'No, no, no, please don't go,' he begged. He'd switched his face from raging bull to wounded puppy.

'What are you doing?' I asked, throwing my hands up with despair.

'I'm sorry, I'm sorry,' he said, rubbing my arms.

I shrugged it off just to keep the peace, but the second our backs were turned he was at it again, shoving another poor innocent clubber.

'We've got to get him out of here,' Lorraine said. I nodded but it was like he'd been listening to our conversation all along.

'I'm sorry, I'm sorry.' He was back, trying to win me over.

Was he playing some sort of game? I looked to Lorraine and she could see the panic and stress in my eyes.

'I'm never going out with you again,' I snapped, glaring at the belt between his clenched hands.

'No, please don't leave me here,' he pleaded.

He followed us into a taxi but I couldn't bear to look at him the whole journey to Lorraine's. I felt angry and scared at the same time. I hadn't seen this aggressive side of Shane and I didn't like it one bit.

'Come on, T, I was just messing around,' he said, poking me in the ribs. His nickname for me was 'T', but now wasn't the time. I held my head in my hands at the thought of what had just happened.

He's drunk, he must just be off his head, I reasoned. He'd never behaved like that before.

Quite a few people we knew at the club had also found their way back to Lorraine's, and her living room and kitchen were taken over by drunks smoking and knocking back cans of beer.

Shane loved being the centre of attention and was fooling around while the mum in me dashed back and forth making sure no one dropped ash onto Lorraine's carpets. Although Shane was busy socialising, I could feel his eyes watching me constantly. When I moved, his eyes moved. I looked behind and he wasn't chatting any more, he was staring right at me.

'Everything all right?' I asked, nervously.

'Uh huh,' he nodded.

I wanted the night to end. It had turned sinister. Lorraine read my mind and pulled me aside.

'I want these people gone,' she hissed. Her mascara had sunk below her eyes and she looked like she could also do with a good night's sleep.

'You want them gone?' Shane cut in. His eyes were wild again.

'Yeah,' Lorraine nodded.

'No problem.' Shane puffed out his chest.

We expected him to tell everyone to leave but instead, to our shock, he pulled back his leg and started booting any men who were sitting on the floor. You could hear the noise of his shoe smacking and scraping across skin.

'Ow, take it easy, mate,' one of them yelped.

'OUT!' he ordered, and started kicking again.

It was chaos. Everyone was scrambling to their feet and making for the door.

What is he doing? I wondered. I cringed as the girls around me screamed.

'Psycho,' someone shouted, making their getaway.

A deathly silence fell over the empty room, as both Lorraine and I were left speechless.

'Well, that got rid of them,' he sniggered.

'You can say that again,' Lorraine snapped. She shot me a troubled look.

I crossed my arms and tapped my foot like an angry parent. He looked up at me through his thick dark eyelashes and I softened. I didn't have the energy to argue at silly o'clock in the morning. I held out my hand and led him to the bed in my sister's spare room, knowing a good night's sleep would make everything better.

Hours later I was woken by Shane's giant body pressing against me. He rolled on top as I was coming around and I knew he wanted sex. He smelled of alcohol and testosterone, as he grinded against me and I allowed my body to mould into his. How could I stay angry with him when he felt this good? I stopped fighting and let him take me.

Shane had a stinking hangover that day but he was back to being the big teddy bear I knew and loved. I'd seen an aggressive side to him but at least it had been targeted at men. Shane's a good guy, he just drinks a bit too much, I told myself. No one's perfect and everyone deserves a second chance. My sister agreed that he was probably way too drunk and assured me it was just a one-off.

But it wasn't just a one-off. Shane's boss didn't forgive him for not showing up to work and he didn't get his job back. Instead of looking for another painting and decorating contract he spent the evenings we were apart partying and the days in bed sleeping off his hangover. I wouldn't have minded so much, but he insisted on ringing me when he was off his face with the sound of girls laughing and squealing in the background. I'd never been one to worry whether my boyfriend was cheating before, but his phone calls were making me feel insecure. He'd ring and then I'd be left guessing what he was up to. Sometimes I wouldn't hear from him for days, by which time I'd imagined the worst. The power in our relationship had shifted – he was now holding the reins and I didn't like that. If I had been honest with myself, I would have acknowledged he was behaving just like my ex.

I busied myself doing the things I usually filled my days with – dropping Ben off at school, taking Liam to nursery, seeing friends, doing the shopping – but my routine was making me feel old and past it, as I imagined the fun Shane was teasing me with. The things I used to love doing were losing their sparkle.

'Come on, Liam, let's go see Nan,' I said, heaving my little boy into my arms. Stopping by Nan's on the way to the village shops had until now been a treat for me. Poor Nan, she must have wondered what the hell was wrong with me because I kept drifting off into my own world as we chatted over tea and cake.

'I swear Liam's growing by the day,' Nan cooed.

Our chitter-chatter about banal things, which I used to find comforting, were now irritating. It wasn't Nan's fault, it was me, I was feeling anxious because of Shane.

'Yes, he's turning into a big man,' I said, lifting him to his feet on my knees. I couldn't let on to Nan that a guy was getting to me.

I thought back to when we were children, and how I used to come home from school and find Mum weeping on the sofa because yet another boyfriend had screwed her around. It was the same old thing every day for a couple of years after her second marriage finished.

'For God's sake,' I'd mutter under my breath as I passed her.

'How can you let yourself get so upset over a guy?' I said, stomping upstairs to my room. I didn't want to comfort her; I despised her for letting herself go.

'I've left your tea there,' Mum would say as I dodged the breakfast table on the way to school. I made a point of retracing my steps, picking up the tea and tipping it down the sink in front of her and her one-night stand.

'You disgust me,' I'd snarl and then walk out. She never said anything. She just carried on making me tea like nothing was wrong.

And here I was, aged twenty-nine, doing exactly that, letting a man get the better of me.

'Do you remember when Granddad used to take all of us to Poole Market at the weekends for gammon, egg and chips?' Nan reminisced, her smiling eyes crinkling at the corners with happiness. I reached out and squeezed her hand lovingly. Nan could always tell when I was feeling down in the dumps.

'Yes, and we'd always stop for cream cake on the way home. And then, we'd have fish and chips for tea.' I remembered our full bellies after a weekend with our grandparents.

I checked my mobile nervously. He still hadn't called. Where is he? I wondered. We were supposed to be seeing each other tonight.

'Another slice of cake, love?' Nan interrupted my thoughts.

I bet he's out with those girls again.

'No, Nan, I'm fine.' I was too anxious to eat.

C'mon, buck up, Nash, I told myself, get on with living your life.

But as much as I wanted to believe my own advice, my life was on hold until I'd heard from Shane. I knew I should cancel our plans for the evening and make my own, but I wanted him so badly I held that window open for him. The waiting was driving me crazy so, after Liam had been picked up by his dad, I headed over to Lorraine's for moral support.

'It's not good enough, Tina,' Lorraine said. Even she, who had been Shane's biggest fan at first, was going off him.

'I know, I know,' I mumbled, curling into her sofa for comfort.

We had dinner and watched some TV together; all the time I kept checking my phone, hoping I'd made a mistake and missed his call. But nothing.

'I'm off to bed now,' Lorraine yawned.

'Night.' I forced a smile.

'Don't wait up for him, Tina,' she warned.

'I won't.'

But that's exactly what I was going to do. I couldn't sleep; my mind was racing with ideas of him cheating on me. I put on DVD after DVD, praying for him to ring. I must have drifted off for a bit because I was woken by the sound of my phone bleating. It was Shane. It was 4.30 a.m.

'I've been out with friends, can I come and see you?' he asked. He didn't sound sorry at all.

'Yeah, come up,' I told him, ringing off.

'Arrgh, you're such an idiot,' I said out loud, screwing my hair up in my hands. I hated myself for letting him come and go as he pleased, but I wanted to see him so badly. I'd missed him. I felt that horrible needy feeling that every girl dreads.

Shane kept me waiting another hour and a half. My stomach somersaulted when I opened the door to him. He was looking dishevelled and as if the hangover had already kicked in, and he smelled of fags and booze. He leaned against the doorframe and rested his head in his arm.

'You gonna let me in?' he asked, staring at me intensely.

I stood back and let him through. Of course I was going to let him in, but I hated myself for being so weak. He slouched onto a chair in the kitchen like he didn't have a care in the world. God, you still look hot even when you're hanging, I thought, as I gazed at his chiselled face.

I sat opposite him. Exhausted.

I cleared my throat. 'Where have you been?' I croaked nervously.

He smirked. He knew he had me just where he wanted me. He said he'd been out with his friends. There were no apologies this time, no explanations; I could tell he was enjoying making me jealous. I tried to fight my corner by telling him his behaviour was not acceptable, but he knew how to hurt me. Out of nowhere he stabbed the knife in.

'I'm with the wrong sister,' he grinned.

I was speechless. I stared at him in disbelief and then my eyes narrowed with anger.

'You prick.' I'd had enough.

'I'm only joking,' he giggled, trying to win back the control. 'I was just seeing what sort of reaction I'd get.' He reached his hand out to me.

I snatched my hand into my chest. I was no longer angry, I just felt very sad. Shane had made me feel really rubbish about myself – I was already feeling down and this made me feel more insecure. The problem was, he'd got under my skin, so when he started being nice to me I felt grateful.

He reached for my hand again and then gently pulled me into his arms. I'd been yearning for that feeling all night. I'd become like a drug addict, only happy when I got my fix – of Shane. I led him into Lorraine's spare room and he lifted me into his big arms and placed me on the bed. Three of me could fit into the size of him, and I felt tiny as I lay beneath his throbbing body. He peeled off his T-shirt to reveal his taut chest and stroked the hair out of my eyes. He was more like the outlaw tattooed on his arm than I realised. There was one rule for him and another for everyone else.

His dark eyes locked onto mine.

'I love you,' he whispered.

My stomach lurched. Those words were like music to my ears. I bit my lower lip to stop myself crying, which would have been embarrassing.

'I love you too,' I said, kissing him.

He then took control, pulling at my clothes, throwing them across the room, while he pressed himself on me, and into me.

'I love you,' he said, moving inside.

'I love you, I love you, I love you.' He wouldn't stop. He must have told me fifty times as we made love. In the end I smothered his mouth with my smiling kiss just to shut him up.

He fell asleep immediately but I lay awake in his arms, staring at the ceiling. I was happy but sad at the same time. Happy I had him back, sad because I'd started to question whether I was actually good enough for him. You'll have to up your game if you want to keep him. You'll have to please him more, I told myself. I was prepared to do whatever it took to keep him from running off again.

4

The Bubble Bursts

'Snow is falling, all around me, children playing, having fun, 'tis the season for love and understanding, Merry Christmas everyone,' I sang to the radio classic at the top of my voice, as I drove my little red Peugeot 306 to Shane's flat in Penzance on Christmas Day 2009.

I'd spent the morning opening presents with my kids, but now it was our special time together. I glanced across to the passenger seat, which was stacked high with gifts I'd carefully wrapped for Shane. We'd only been together four months but I wanted to impress him. Had I bought enough? I suddenly panicked. It was too late now; I'd arrived outside his place.

'Merry Christmas, T,' he said with a big goofy grin on his face.

He behaved just like a kid sometimes, which brought out my mothering instinct.

'No, don't feel your presents,' I squealed, hiding them behind my back as I side-stepped my way into his flat.

I gasped. It was like I'd stepped into Santa's grotto. His living room was covered top to toe in tinsel and flashing lights and hanging stars and balloons.

'I've done this for you,' he said proudly.

I tried to speak but the words trapped in my throat. I'd never seen anything like it. It was completely over the top.

'It's lovely.' I squeezed his hand.

Beneath the Christmas tree was a heap of presents waiting for me to unwrap. I handed him his, and he scooped up my bundle and tipped them on my lap.

'Present opening time,' he giggled.

The only sound that could be heard for the next few minutes was of wrapping paper being torn apart.

'No way,' I yelped with delight, as I held up a pair of Nike Air Max trainers. Shane had spent a small fortune on me. He'd also given me a pair of pyjamas and a hooded black jumper by a trendy surfing brand.

'It's adorable,' I squealed again, as I unwrapped a teddy bear holding a heart with 'I Love You' scrawled across it. I buried my nose into its fur, which Shane had doused with his aftershave.

'So I don't forget you?' I joked. I looked across to see how he was getting on, as I hadn't heard a peep out of him. He was sitting deathly quiet with a mountain of wrapping paper burying his feet.

'Do you like your presents?' I asked him, panicking slightly.

'Yes,' he replied, and nodded. He was behaving like he'd never been given a gift before and he didn't know what to do.

'Thank you so much, Shane, for all my lovely presents.' I tried to bring him back out of his shell. He smiled shyly and it made me want to wrap him up in my arms. He was like a little lost boy who I needed to rescue.

I'd given him a bottle of Amaretto, so we cracked that open and mixed it with some orange juice.

'Merry Christmas,' I said, toasting Shane. 'And to many more to come.' I winked as we clinked glasses. Part of me was joking, but my heart was telling me after years of trying I'd met 'the one'. We didn't spend much longer in his place as he'd promised to take me to his dad's for afternoon drinks. Shane had told me a little about William, that he was a taxi driver but used to be in the Royal Marines. He said his mum and dad had divorced when Shane was thirteen and Shane had spent some years in the care of social services. I left his past well alone, as speaking about it made him withdraw.

'My dad taught me it was important to stick up for myself in school,' Shane volunteered, as we made our way down to his dad's flat in the town centre.

'Oh, right,' I listened.

'This kid beat me up one time and when I told Dad he made me get in his car and he drove us around the streets until we found him.'

'And then what?' I asked, concerned.

'Then he told me to get out and beat the shit out of him,' he replied. His face was emotionless.

'Did you?' I swallowed my words.

'Yeah.' Shane shrugged like it was nothing.

There was an awkward silence for the rest of the way, and I was relieved when we arrived at William's. I was expecting a big brute of a man, given Shane's size and with him having been in the Marines, but I couldn't have been more wrong.

'Merry Christmas, son,' answered a little silver-haired man half the height of his son. Behind him stood his girlfriend Hayley, who must have been at least ten years younger than he was. He's done well, I thought to myself.

'Hello,' he greeted me, giving me a kiss. His face was tanned and weather-beaten, each wrinkle with a story to tell. William came across as a nice guy. He'd gone out of his way to buy me and my boys some stocking fillers. He'd got Liam a toy duck for the bath and Ben a puzzle.

'You shouldn't have,' I giggled, as I unwrapped some false nails and nail varnish. Shane must have let on that I liked my grooming.

We drank beer and listened to William's war stories. He talked about his hair-raising patrols and his days as a dog-handler for the Army. I struggled to believe the things I had been told about William, he seemed so nice.

'Essence of the world,' Shane said, holding his pint glass high into the air. I rolled my eyes, as that was his favourite saying when we were out.

'Prick in a glass,' William cut him down. There was clearly some tension, but I wasn't there to read into Shane's childhood. I just wanted to enjoy my first Christmas with my boyfriend.

Christmas 2009 was turning out to be one of the best I'd had in a long time. Shane was ringing regularly, making me feel wanted, and the anxiety that had built up over the past month was dying down. So when Shane insisted we go to Poldark Mine for a rave on New Year's Eve I was reluctant. There was always trouble when we went partying, and I'd worked out we were best one-on-one.

It was Shane's first time to the rave in the grounds of an old tin mine in Truro. We drove there with a couple of his friends and his eyes lit up when he stepped into the party, which is like a underground village with music banging out from every building. He puffed up his chest to play the hard man, as he was no longer a big fish in a small pool with this crowd.

'Woo-hoo,' I screamed, jumping around on the spot. The atmosphere was electric.

'Come on, Shane, let's go dancing,' I said, punching the air with my hand. Shane scowled as he was pushed by the throbbing crowd.

'I'm going to the bar,' he signalled, and I mouthed I'd wait for him as he disappeared into the throng.

I spent the rest of the night trying to find him. Luckily I ran into his sister's boyfriend, Nick, who I ended up celebrating the New Year with, otherwise I would have been all alone.

'There you are,' I said with relief, as I finally found Shane at the exit to the mine. His arms were folded, his mouth snarly like a dog. He looked very pissed off.

'Where have you been?' I said, going up to him for a kiss.

'You fucking slut,' he hissed.

Did he just call me a slut? I couldn't believe it.

'What?' I was gobsmacked.

'You fucking slut,' he repeated, spit flying. 'I've been out here all night. You couldn't give a shit because you've been in there flirting with every fucking man. I bet you were fucking them too.'

I was speechless. No one had ever spoken to me like this in my life.

'I didn't even know you were in there,' I mumbled with shock, backing up against the wall.

He made a strange gargling noise, tilted his head back, and then spat on me.

'Fucking slut,' he said, as I wiped his spit off my face in disbelief. He did it again, and again, he was firing spit at me like a machine gun.

'Stop it,' I pleaded in fear and embarrassment. He was making me feel worthless.

'Hey, ease up, mate.' His friend stepped in but Shane was an 'outlaw' and didn't listen to anyone. He kept firing at me and I cowered against the wall, covering my face with my hands.

'Bitch,' he spat. He then turned and marched off arrogantly to wait by his friend's car for his lift home. We were so far from Penzance I had no choice but to take the ride with him. His friend signalled me to jump in the front seat while Shane clambered into the back. Steam was coming off him, he was so angry. I could feel his dark eyes boring into me, hating me, as I sat quietly in front, totally confused by what I'd done wrong.

'Poldark was good this year,' one of his friends said, trying to lighten the mood.

'SLAG!' Shane interrupted and then yanked my hair through the headrest.

'Owww,' I yelped, caressing the burn.

'Slut,' he hissed again. He then spat on me once more.

I was helpless and his friends were too terrified to stick up for me. Please hurry up, please hurry up, I thought, bowing my head in desperation to get home. Had he been taking drugs? I couldn't understand where this anger was coming from.

'Shut up!' I covered my ears with my hands. I didn't know how else to escape the firing line. I withdrew into myself and tried to block out his taunts the best I could. There was no way

I was going to spend the night around his place now. I broke the news to Shane seconds before we pulled up at his flat.

'I'm getting my things,' I demanded, now fuming from the way he'd humiliated me.

Shane slung another insult at me, before casually getting out of the car and swaggering to his front door. I stood nervously next to him, fidgeting, as I waited for him to unlock the door. The key turned and then he turned on me. Shane lurched forward, pushing me with his powerful arms. My feet lifted off the ground and I went flying to the road. WHACK! My head smacked the concrete as I fell onto my back. Pain shot through me and I lay there cradling my concussion for a moment. What the hell just happened? Then the survival adrenaline kicked in. I scurried to my feet and pushed past Shane, darting into his flat. I frantically gathered up all my clothes and essentials into my arms and ran past him again as he followed after me. I jumped head first into the back seat of his friend's car.

'GO, GO!' I screamed.

His friend revved the engine and screeched off. I looked out the back window and saw Shane sprinting up the road after me.

'BITCH!' he yelled, shaking his fists in the air. I slumped down into the seat, my heart racing at a hundred miles an hour.

'You OK?' his friend asked, also in shock.

'Yeah,' I lied. I couldn't compute what just happened. It was too much for my throbbing head to process. I asked to be dropped off at my best friend Danielle's house in town. I'd feel safe there, as she didn't take any crap from men and would help fend Shane off if he came looking for me.

'Oh crap, I left my car outside his house.' I stamped my foot down, terrified at the thought of another run-in with my so-called boyfriend.

'I'll come with you,' Danielle volunteered. 'Not having you go through that alone.' I could tell she was holding back from telling me 'I told you so', as she was the one who had originally warned me off Shane ten years ago.

My heart was in my mouth as we turned the corner into Shane's street the following evening. It was dark and freezing and I could see my own nervous breath puffing in front of me. 'Please don't let him see me, please don't let him see me,' I muttered under my breath.

'What did you say?' Danielle craned her head to hear my murmurs.

'Nothing . . .' I started, but I was stopped mid-sentence.

'Nooooooo,' I screamed. Someone had thrown a brick through my windscreen, shattering it into a thousand cracks.

'He did this, I know he did this,' I repeated, shaking my head with distress. My car was my life. I didn't have much money and I'd spent years saving up for it. Danielle grabbed my hand from my face and tried to calm me down.

'You need to get it out of here before he totally trashes it,' she said calmly, trying to focus me. My head was still throbbing from the knock yesterday, and spinning from everything that had happened. I felt scared and checked up and down the street to make sure Shane wasn't about to pounce on me.

'Now, Tina,' Danielle ordered. There was no messing with her.

I got behind the wheel, terrified the splintered glass would rain down shards at any second. I couldn't see a thing, so I drove at snail speed with my head hanging out the side window. I stashed my Peugeot up a side street to be collected at a later date.

'Let's get out of here,' I said to Danielle, fighting back the tears. How could things have gone so downhill in the space of twenty-four hours? I wanted answers. I needed to have my say.

I didn't have to wait long. I was back at my sister's and Lorraine had just handed me a cup of tea when my mobile went off. It was Shane.

'Hello?' I picked up on the last ring. I was bubbling with rage. He'd humiliated me and trashed my car. I hated him.

All I could hear was the familiar noise of girls giggling and glasses clinking in the background. Shane was back partying, trying to make me jealous, but it wasn't going to work this time.

'Did you brick my car?' I barked.

'Ha, ha, ha,' Shane erupted in laughter. 'Yeah,' he slurred before hanging up.

There was no sorry, no remorse, no 'please forgive me'. I couldn't believe he was treating me with such little respect. Was I worth so little? I couldn't believe I was asking myself that question. Problem was, I was starting to think it.

'He trashed my effing car,' I relayed to Lorraine. Mum used to smack us if we swore, so I held my tongue even under the most extreme circumstances.

'He's off with those girls again,' I carried on. 'He had the cheek to call me a slut, but I bet he's doing all sorts with them.'

The thought made me sick, because however much I hated him right now, I also wanted the Shane I knew to come back to me. The soft Shane who told me he loved me.

The next forty-eight hours were hell. I morphed from the tough surfer chick that everyone knew to a pathetic needy doormat that checked her mobile every five minutes wishing Shane would call. If I wasn't checking my phone I was looking on Facebook to see what he was up to. I felt he was tormenting me by changing his profile picture to one of him with an arm around a tarty girl with her cleavage on display, fake tan, long dark hair, and fake nails curled around a champagne glass.

'I'm going to get wrecked tonight!' he updated his status. He was trying to wind me up. I was sure of it and it was bloody working. Meanwhile, I had turned into my mum – I couldn't move from the sofa because I'd let a guy control my emotions. I wouldn't eat I was so anxious and I couldn't stop crying.

'I don't recognise you, Tine?' Lorraine said, offering me a hug.

I pulled the quilt up to my neck and curled into the armrest. I felt horrible and ugly and Shane was the only one who could make it better.

Please call, please call . . .

'Come on, Tine, he ain't worth it,' Lorraine said, trying to pull me out from my misery. But I had started to believe I was as worthless as how Shane treated me.

I was so down that I asked Paul to look after the kids for the three days I was with Lorraine – I couldn't have them seeing me like this. By day five I was about to tear my hair out for there was still no word from Shane. I was washing up when there was a rap at the front door. My hands froze beneath the soap suds as my gut told me it was him. I'd been waiting so long for this moment but now I wasn't sure I wanted it. I knew that whatever followed it was going to be on his terms, because he was now in the driving seat. He was no longer chasing me; I was putty in his hands.

'You've got to help me,' he blurted out when I opened the door. His eyes were wild and frantic.

'I've got Lithuanians after me,' he said, looking over his shoulder up the road.

'What?' I asked.

'I smashed a whisky bottle in someone's face and now they're all after me.' His big body was jittery.

What had he done? My heart was racing for him. He'd successfully glossed over his apology with his drama.

'Come in, then,' I said, leading him out of danger. He paced the room, his arms flying up and back down to his side. The crowds he mingled with were so different to mine I had no idea what sort of trouble he was in. I had found his other life attractive to begin with but now it scared me.

He turned on his heels and blasted at me.

'None of this would have happened if you hadn't left me on New Year.' He was blaming me.

'What? How is this my fault?'

'It's all your fault,' he said, his eyes wild again. 'If we'd never argued, I'd never have got in a fight and now these Lithuanians want to kill me,' he shouted, like it all made perfect sense. He was so convincing, maybe it was partly my fault? Maybe I wound him up too much? How could I fix it? My heart was racing again.

'I'm sorry,' I mumbled.

He paused for a moment and I was back on tenterhooks waiting for what he would say next.

'That's better,' he said, smiling.

Shane seemed to calm down after that and he wanted to touch me again, this time with his gentle hands. I was so happy to have him back in my arms that I shoved aside my worries for that evening. I didn't even dare ask who he had been with in those past five days. Had he slept with that tart in the picture? I couldn't bear the thought of setting him off again so I kept my thoughts to myself and my mouth firmly shut.

'Children should be seen and not heard.' My mum's words invaded my head. I'd learned the hard way what the punishment for opening my mouth was when I was a kid and I was quickly learning the same lesson from Shane.

We made passionate love that night. The make-up sex with him was ten times more intense than I'd ever experienced before. He was slow and loving and looked at me like he wanted to own my soul. He locked his fingers between mine and raised them above my head as he moved inside. 'I love you,' he said, as he squeezed my hand, tighter, and tighter, until we both groaned with ecstasy.

I was on a high all morning after Shane left but, just like a hangover, the horrible feeling started to kick in. I felt hollow inside, like someone had died – but it wasn't Shane who had gone, it was me. Old Tina was quickly fading into a washed-out version, but I didn't know how to get her back. I hated myself for being so weak and forgiving Shane, but our love was fast becoming a drug.

A day later he was back on my doorstep. It was as if he could tell I was having doubts about him. He was looking frantic again and was hiding something behind his back. Had he brought me flowers? My heart jumped with hope that he finally had an apology.

'What you got there?' I asked, trying to pull out his hands.

He edged his way with his back up against the wall into my living room and then pulled out his surprise.

'Oh my God, that looks like a bloody gun!' I shouted, jumping back.

He was grinning like a Cheshire cat, as he held out a massive crossbow that looked like a shotgun, only more threatening.

'To protect me,' he said, matter-of-factly.

I'd never seen anything like it in my life. I was delving into an underworld I didn't have a clue about and I was lost for words. I glanced back at it from the corner of my eye. It was exactly like a shotgun with a big barrel and a trigger, only it had a steel bow at the end. Shane was excited by his new toy, which he claimed was going to save his life from a gang of Lithuanians. It was so heavy he had to rest it on the floor as he pulled the wire back to set the trigger.

'You have to watch your fingers or the wire will take them off when it fires,' he said with glee.

'What are you doing?'

I looked on with horror as he continued to load it. I imagined the wire slicing off his fingers like cheese.

'Let me show you,' he said. 'Can I shoot it from your back window into your shed?'

'NO! No bloody way!' I shook my head violently. What was he thinking?

I told him to get it the hell out of my house. The kids weren't in but what if they had been? What was he thinking? None of this seemed real – lethal crossbows, being hunted down by Lithuanians. It was like something out of a film. I was feeling shaky, so I called Lorraine after I'd got Shane to take it home with him.

'What an idiot,' Lorraine said. I could feel her eyes rolling with exasperation at the other end of the line.

'It's always when we go out that he gets himself into trouble,' I reasoned. 'He's not normally like that with me.' I justified New Year's Eve. I'd convinced myself that only I had the power to unlock the good in him.

'I don't know what spell he's put you under,' Lorraine snapped.

She was right – the nastier and scarier he was the more scared I was to lose him.

5

The Nightmare Begins

'You're already massive. Why do you need to take steroids?'
I looked at Shane's body in despair.

He shook the jar of M1T which his friend had ordered on the internet for £40. It's such a potent testosterone booster, it has been banned in the USA.

'Down the hatch.' He washed the big red capsule away with a glug of beer.

Shane was a law unto himself. And it seemed like he was rubbing my nose in his outlaw behaviour. It was as if he wanted me to fear him.

'I thought steroids make you aggressive,' I quizzed.

Shane puffed out his chest like he had just swallowed the strength of ten men.

'Don't worry, T, I just want to gain another stone and this will help me,' he said, flexing his muscles.

'But everything you've done so far, you've done without steroids. So why do you want to take them now?' I badgered. 'I really don't think it's a good idea to mess with these.'

'Stop fussing,' he said, cutting me short. He then went on about the extra weights he was going to be able to bench-press at the gym, thanks to his magic pills.

I was quickly learning that the best way to get on with Shane was not to answer back. We settled down in front of a DVD that night. His choice as usual – yet another zombie film. I'd no idea when I first met him how much he was into horror films, but that's all he seemed to watch and play on his games console. I was faced with blood and guts on my TV screen almost every day, as Shane had practically moved in over the two months since New Year.

He still hadn't found a job, so we were spending a lot of time together. I found it suffocating but it was also making my feelings for him more intense. My skin tingled as Shane stroked my arm and I stroked his hand affectionately – it was our ritual we always had when watching films together. We would bicker and then make up, bicker and then make up. I couldn't live with him but I couldn't live without him.

That night I dreamed of his crossbow.

I was running through a tunnel but my legs couldn't keep up and I fell on my hands and knees, scraping my skin back.

I screamed in pain at the blood pouring from my knees. I wobbled to my feet like a newborn calf and started running again into the dark hole. I looked around and Shane was chasing me with his crossbow.

'No, Shane, I'm not one of them,' I pleaded, trying to make him understand I wasn't a zombie.

'You're evil,' he snarled, catching up with me.

I fell to the floor again, grit sliding into my palms. Shane was metres away now. I watched in horror as he pulled back the arrow and took aim. I scrambled to my feet and I heard the trigger as he fired into my back.

* * *

'No, Shane,' I screamed, waking up bolt upright in bed. I couldn't breathe; sweat was dripping down my neck, back and chest. I looked across, worried I may have woken Shane, but he was sleeping like a baby. I pulled my sweaty blonde hair off my face into a ponytail and lay back down again. If I believed in what dreams tell you then I should be worried for my life. Don't be silly, Tina, it's just a dream, I told myself so I could get back to sleep.

The next two weeks went brilliantly and it was like when we first got together. I was just starting to relax, when Shane turned on me again.

We were meeting his dad for a drink in the London pub in Penzance. Despite what Shane had said about him, I liked his father, so I was looking forward to it. It was my round for drinks and I started chatting to an old lady at the bar while I ordered. She had a thick Cockney accent and a fun cheeky personality, so we got on like a house on fire.

'This pub hasn't changed a bit,' started the seventy-year-old.

'Oh, right?' I was ready to hear her nostalgic story when I felt Shane's massive body lurking behind me. No doubt hurrying me up for the drinks, I thought.

'You trying to get it on with my girlfriend?' he barked at the old lady.

The old lady stumbled back, startled.

'Do you think she's a lesbian?' he leered. The poor old lady didn't know what to say as Shane towered over her. Her lip quivered and she looked to me for help.

'What the hell?' I snapped. What did he think he was doing, speaking to an old woman like that?

'Do you like grannies now?' he chuckled to me.

The whole pub fell silent, as a guy got up and approached Shane.

'Oi, what the hell are you playing at? This ain't on!' he said, fearlessly pointing his finger of disgust at Shane.

I saw the river of red run up Shane's neck and bleed into his face. He blinked and then his eyes turned into black marble. It was like I was watching it happen in slow motion but I couldn't find the pause button to stop it. He wound back his fist and lurched forward.

'I'm going to kick your head in,' he said to the guy, and the old lady ducked for her life.

'Shane, no, Shane, no,' came a dozen voices in chorus, as everyone ran out of nowhere to pin him back. His dad grabbed his arms as he fought like a fish caught on a hook. His macho display made me sick.

'This is a joke,' I said, as I grabbed my handbag and stormed out the pub.

I stomped down the hill with my arms crossed and looked up the street to see lots of commotion. People were shouting, diving in and out of the pub. All I could hear was Shane's name being shouted like he was a celebrity.

'Idiot!' I shouted at him, but also at myself for liking him.

I glanced back up and saw Shane diving out of the pub, his T-shirt half hanging off him. He looked like a mad bull that had been let out of the ring. He scanned the street and then his eyes locked on me like a missile.

I turned and started running, just like in my dream, but two bounds and he was on my back. He pushed me into a dark alley using his body as a barricade to stop me escaping.

'What the hell are you doing?' I trembled, trying to get past him, but he pushed me back. I tried again and he pushed me to the ground. My heart was racing; I was literally cornered like a trapped animal. Shane's face was snarly but his eyes were black and emotionless. I scrambled to my hands and knees and threw myself onto the fence behind me. I tried to climb it but Shane grabbed my leg and yanked me to the ground with a crash.

'Ouch,' I yelped in pain, as my skin stripped off underneath my jeans. I was now on all fours, panting from fear and for air. Shane started coming for me again but somehow I managed to get to my feet and swerve my tiny body past the giant. Finally I had the advantage being small. I ran back into the main street and down the hill as fast as my aching legs could carry me.

Being a small town, Shane's friend Antoine was walking past and tried to grab hold of me.

'Are you OK?' he asked. He must have been able to see my heart jumping out of my chest. I was in too much shock to speak. We both looked around to see Shane running out of the alley after me, and then he stopped dead as he saw someone had got to me first.

'I'm going home,' I shouted with the tiny strength I had left.

Shane looked at my chaperone and backed off.

I went straight to Lorraine's for moral support. She was the only one of my family who had met Shane so far and she was the one who had seen his nice side when we met him in a club six months ago. I'd stopped shaking by the time I saw her – I was now angry.

'He thinks he's a tough guy but it's all talk,' I said to Lorraine, as I paced up and down her living room with a cigarette in my hand. I had started smoking heavily again to calm my nerves.

'Tine, you do not want to be messing with him,' Lorraine warned.

'I can't believe he said that to an old lady,' I said, throwing my hands in the air. I took another drag of the cigarette while I continued to have a conversation with my conscience. 'And then chasing me down the street and pushing me around like that.

'But he's not normally like that, Lorraine,' I said, turning to her. 'It's been amazing for the past two weeks, he's been fine. It's when he goes out, that's when all the problems start.'

'There's no excuse for that kind of behaviour,' Lorraine tried to reason.

I took another long drag on the cigarette, as my mind whirred. I kept coming back to the same reasoning – that he was different when he was with me. That he was all right *really*.

I turned to my sister; my eyes were now wild and frantic. 'Maybe I bring the worst out in him? Maybe it's my fault?'

'What?' she mouthed.

'He's pushed me around but he hasn't hit me, Lorraine,' I argued.

'He went nuts on his neighbour who was beating up his girlfriend.'

'He doesn't hit girls, only guys,' I said.

I was certain of it.

6

True Colours

'No, Shane, nooooo!' I screamed. I'd never screamed like that in my life. I sounded like a baby yelling its head off.

This time I wasn't dreaming. Shane was pressing his thumbs into my eyes with the force of his whole body. The pain was indescribable as he pushed deeper and harder. I thought my eyes were going to go into my brain.

'Arrghhh!' My scream turned into a gargle.

Twelve hours earlier, things couldn't have been more different. It was a scorching sunny day, unusually hot for April, so I'd headed straight into the garden to sunbathe. I jumped onto the kids' trampoline at the back of the yard and stretched myself across it. I shut my eyes with happiness as the warm rays heated me up.

This is the life, I thought. I might not have much money but I have two beautiful children, I live in one of the most beautiful parts of the country, I have amazing friends and I'm in love.

Things had been incredible between Shane and me over the past few weeks and I was having feelings like he could be the person I would spend my life with. I spread my arms out like a starfish, lapping up the warmth and my warm thoughts.

I turned my head and looked through the living-room window at Shane, who'd just woken up and was crouched down, setting up the Xbox to play computer games. Ben was at school and Liam was at his dad's, so we had the day to ourselves – I'll get him into the garden, I thought.

The hours ticked past, my tan had deepened, but Shane was still indoors playing virtual football. How could he not want to be in the sunshine? I waited to catch his attention and then beckoned him onto my trampoline. He shook his head and then returned his gaze to the wide screen.

He needs to get a job, I thought. Playing these computer games all day isn't healthy. He should also get back into his rugby. I was convinced if he had more going on in his life then his angry outbursts would stop. He was a big boy and needed something to get his teeth stuck into. The mum in me came out.

'Yessss!' Shane cheered, as he scored a goal just as I walked through the living room to answer the front door. It was Kate, an old friend of Lorraine's; we'd all grown up on the estate together.

'All right?' I asked. She also had the same idea about sunbathing. I led her and her kids into the back garden. Shane barely looked up from his game; he was still engrossed.

'Don't mind him,' I joked, and then pulled up a garden chair for my friend. Not long after, we were joined by Kate's boyfriend, who came and sat next to us.

'How nice is this?' I said, looking up to the sun, basking in happiness. There was someone missing from this picture though. I turned around and signalled to Shane again to join us.

'Come and have a drink with us,' I said.

'Nah, I'm playing,' he grunted.

Miserable bugger, I thought.

More hours passed. Ben came back from school and Liam was dropped off by his dad.

'Pssst, why don't we go for a drink down the pub and the boys can look after the kids?' Kate suggested with a twinkle in her eye.

I rarely went to the pub, and Kate was being her most persuasive.

'Why not,' I said with a nod. Sometimes in life you've just got to be spontaneous. I wouldn't have done it if Shane wasn't happy with baby-sitting though. I didn't want to upset him.

'Yeah, that's fine,' he said. It was 8.30 p.m. and the kids were already in bed, so he could just carry on with his video games. He'd been playing them for near enough ten hours now. Kate's boyfriend took her kids back home while we headed off to the local.

There was a biting chill in the air by now, and Kate slung on her jacket over her strappy top. She was wearing hot pants over tights and heels. The pub was two minutes down the road, just past the turning to my nan's house. It was nice chatting to Kate, as she was like an old family friend.

'Vodka?' she suggested with a mischievous grin.

I sighed deeply. I should have seen this coming.

'All right.' I went along with it.

Countless drinks later I was swaying all over the place. I didn't drink much, let alone vodka. For some reason we thought it would be a good idea to stop in on my nan, who also knew Kate well. We stumbled up the road, holding on to each other in fits of giggles.

'Hi, Nan,' I said, drooping on her doorstep.

Nan wasn't quite so pleased to see me this time. She had her son Glen and his friend in. They were settled down in front of the TV and, not surprisingly, didn't feel in the mood for entertaining me.

'Go home,' she ordered firmly.

'Sorry, Nan,' I giggled, and Kate sniggered beside me. Nan asked my uncle's friend to walk me up the road and I left Kate behind. I can't remember much about the getting home, apart from that it seemed to take forever.

'Put her to bed,' I heard the friend tell Shane at my front door. Everything looked blurred. I felt sick.

'Look at the state of you,' Shane said, grabbing hold of my arms before I fell to the floor. He hauled me up the stairs and threw me down on my bed, which was still just a mattress on the floor. That was the last thing I remember before passing out into a deep drunken slumber.

It must have been 2 a.m. when I came round. Was that music coming from downstairs? I rolled off my bed and listened in to the tunes blasting from the front room. What the hell? My kids were trying to sleep. I stamped on the floor to tell Shane to turn it down.

Shane bounded up the stairs wearing his usual tracksuit bottoms and black-and-white striped Pirates rugby shirt.

'What? What?' he barked.

'Look at the state of you, you've been sick all over yourself,' he pointed in disgust.

I turned around to see a pool of vomit across the bed sheets. I gasped. My head was pounding. I went downstairs to clean myself up and then walked into the living room.

'What the bloody hell has been going on here?' I said, staring at Kate, who was asleep in just her top and underwear on my sofa. She must have followed after I left Nan's. One look and it was pretty obvious what had been going on – my boyfriend had been fooling around with my supposed friend.

A fire lit inside my gut. Enough is enough, no man cheats on me. It was my turn to bound up the stairs full of rage to where Shane was still waiting in my bedroom.

'I know what's gone on here,' I spat. 'Get out of my house now,' I ordered.

Shane's eyes turned black. He looked like a robot about to exterminate someone – me.

SMACK!

He punched me in the face, sending me into a spin. What the hell? I didn't know what was happening. I turned to face him again.

SMACK!

To the other cheek, with all the power of his body. I don't know how I was still standing.

SMACK! Around the back of my head.

My ear felt like it had exploded. The whole room fell quiet and all I could hear was myself breathing. I dropped to my knees on my mattress and pulled the duvet cover over my head like a child hiding from a monster. I could hear his footsteps getting closer. I pulled the duvet tightly around me. *Please help me, God!*

Shane ripped the duvet off me and flipped me onto my back. He jumped on top and pinned me down with his giant eighteen-stone body. I looked into his eyes and they were black and emotionless like the Grim Reaper.

He put his thumbs into my eyes and tried to push them into my head.

I screamed like a wailing baby. I'd never felt pain like it. The pressure was indescribable. He meant it; he wanted to blind me.

It felt like he was there forever but it was probably ten seconds before I found the warrior inside me. I called on the strength I used to control those show horses when I was a kid, and kicked him off me. I scrambled to my feet and ran for my bedroom door.

Run, Tina, run for your life! I could hear my heart pound in my ears.

I wasn't fast enough. Shane pounced on me from behind, lifted me up, and threw me into my kid's bedroom next door.

I landed in a heap on the floor between Ben's bed and Liam's cot. The boys woke up and Liam started crying while Ben looked terrified. I couldn't move, every inch of my body felt on fire. I lay there panting, just trying to stay alive. I heard a trickling noise and then the flush of the upstairs toilet.

I couldn't believe it – he was taking a piss in the middle of beating the shit out of me?!

I had to get out of the kids' room, I couldn't let them see him hit me again. I crawled on my hands and knees to the door and I felt his hands on me again. He lifted me up and chucked me down the stairs.

I tumbled all the way down and landed in the hallway like a limp rag doll. I didn't know where I was, the room was spinning and my vision was blurred. All I could feel was intense shooting pain in my fingers. I used the wall to slide back onto my feet and I stumbled into the living room for help. I held my dislocated thumbs up in front of me.

'He's beat the shit out of me!' I cried for the first time. But Kate had gone. She had left me with the monster.

I stumbled around in a daze and then walked out into my front garden, sobbing. I had no idea if Shane was about to pounce again.

'What's happened, love?' yelled my neighbour Zara, who must have heard my screams, from her upstairs window.

'He's just beaten the shit out of me,' I repeated, walking in circles around my garden.

Zara came flying down the stairs to my rescue. Her face dropped as she saw my injuries. They must have been horrific.

'Oh my God, Tina, look at the state of your face,' she said, scared to touch me.

'My kids, my kids,' I screeched. My injuries could wait. I needed to get them out of the house.

Shane appeared at the front door just as I managed to scramble up onto Zara's wall out of danger. He swaggered into the yard like he owned the place. His face and eyes were back to normal but he'd turned ugly in my eyes. He wasn't human.

'Get the hell out of my house!' I growled at him from Zara's wall.

The skin on my face was getting tighter by the second as it swelled up. One pop and I thought it would explode. He stood there arrogantly with his hands in his jogging bottoms. I don't think he could quite believe I was chucking him out.

'Get out,' I said again. I don't know how my body was still functioning.

Zara weaved past him to grab my kids while he stood there staring daggers at me. He then leaned forward and stuck the knife in.

'You deserved a kicking,' he chuckled.

'GET OUT OF MY HOUSE!' I screamed. I couldn't bear to look at his demonic face any longer.

He stomped inside like a child who'd had his toy taken away from him and then proceeded to remove all his things from my house. First his beloved TV, then his horror DVDs. The last hour had been something straight out of one of his sick films.

'Slag,' he hissed, trying to spit on me as he walked past.

Zara came out carrying Liam in one arm and holding Ben with her other hand. Ben looked at me with big watery eyes. I bit my lip. I couldn't cry, I had to stay strong for them.

'It's going to be OK, Mummy's fine,' I lied. I knew Shane wouldn't hurt them but I couldn't let them see my battered face for any length of time.

Shane kept charging in and out, piling his things up in the middle of the road like a crazy person.

'I know something happened with Kate, I'm not stupid,' I said. For some reason the fact he had disrespected me in my own house burned more than my injuries.

'Yeah, I did sleep with her,' he sniggered. But a few seconds later he panicked. 'No, I didn't, I'm only messing around,' he backtracked.

Once he'd moved all his things into the road he sat there

hurling abuse at me. He'd be vile and then nice, nasty, then apologetic. My head was spinning.

'We've called the police, they're on their way,' I lied, hoping that would make him run. I hadn't called the police because I was afraid of what Shane would do to me if I told the Old Bill the truth. Moreover, the thought of getting him in trouble made me feel guilty because I didn't want to be the one to send him back to prison.

After nearly four hours of listening to his rants, Zara assured me Shane wouldn't leave of his own accord and we needed help. I told her to do it, although I had no idea what sort of can of worms I was opening. I was now delirious with the pain.

I was still sitting on the wall, soaking up Shane's tirade, when the flashing blue lights of the police cars lit up the sleeping street. Shane rose to his feet, rolled up his sleeves and puffed out his chest. The police officers didn't notice me at first and walked straight up to Shane and his heap in the road.

'What's going on here?' the officer asked.

Shane crossed his arms and played the tough guy.

'Nothing,' he lied.

They then turned around and clocked me, and their expressions changed to horror.

'Who's done that to your face?' they choked.

The warrior in me rose up again. 'He did,' I said, pointing at Shane. His face dropped as if to say 'Oh my God, you are actually grassing me up'. He clearly thought I would keep my mouth shut. The police officers lurched for him and cuffed his hands behind his back. He kept his eyes on me the whole way through, watching me, intimidating me. As they frogmarched him to the car he craned his neck around and stared, never taking his eyes off me until they pushed his head down.

I let out a massive sigh. I had no idea I'd been holding my breath. I looked at my hands and they were trembling. A woman police officer eased me down from the wall and wrapped a blanket around me. She asked if I would make a statement at the police station next to Nan's house. I nodded. The fire inside me was quickly turning to embers.

The police station was very basic with whitewashed walls and the sort of tables and chairs you find in school classrooms. It was 6 a.m. now, and the sun was making itself known through the blinds. The policewoman pulled out a form and poised her pen ready to take my statement. I clasped my hands together to stop them shaking, my whole body was now trembling from the adrenalin, from the pain.

I was scared – I'd never been beaten up before. I've never been involved with the police in my life. I didn't know what making a statement would lead to. I kept wiping the tears from my eyes as I told her my horror story. She explained that Shane had been arrested and charged with causing grievous bodily harm, and he would be kept in the cells until tomorrow when he would appear before the local magistrates.

She then stopped and grabbed my trembling hands. 'You really need to go to hospital, your face is a mess,' she said softly.

'Really?' I had no idea. I still hadn't seen the injuries.

'We think your cheekbone is broken.' She tried not to alarm me as she said it.

I touched my cheek and a shooting pain bounced through the

bones in my face. My hands trembled again, as I imagined a disfigured mess. I was too scared to look in the mirror. The lady called an ambulance and ten minutes later I was puffing on gas and air, as I was rushed into A&E.

I was given a bed in a cubicle, as the overworked doctor darted back and forth between me and his other emergency patients. As I lay there, all alone, my armour finally came crashing down, as the enormity of what had just happened hit me. It was time to finally see the damage. I hooked my exhausted legs off the bed and shuffled to the toilet; three deep breaths and then I forced my head to turn to the mirror.

'Oh my God,' I whispered.

Tears welled in my eyes and burned my skin as they trickled down my blue face. I didn't recognise the hideous monster looking back at me. My eyes were black and swollen, one side of my face looked like it didn't have a cheekbone any more. My lips were puffed and bloody like I'd been stung by a hundred bees. Dried blood was smeared across my face in every direction.

'Why?' I whimpered, as I touched my face with trembling hands.

The tears gushed from my eyes. It was the first time I'd let myself really cry and I couldn't make them stop.

'I can't believe you have done this to me,' I said aloud as my sliced lip wobbled. No man had ever beaten me before and I couldn't get my head around it.

'Why? Why?' I sobbed. I cried so hard I couldn't breathe.

I thought he loved me. The pain in my heart hurt more than my face.

I made my way back to my cubicle and collapsed on my bed.

I'd never felt so low, so depressed as at that moment. 'You ugly stupid piece of shit,' I spat at myself. Shane had made me feel ugly on the inside as well as the outside and not worthy of anyone's love.

After several long hours alone I was allowed to go home. I never wanted my mother, but I needed her right now. I picked up the phone and dialled the woman whom I vowed I'd never become.

'Pick up, pick up,' I chanted. Please.

'Hello?' Mum's familiar voice sent me over the edge.

'Mum, I'm in hospital,' I stuttered.

'What?' Her voice screeched with panic.

'I've been beaten up,' I managed, before breaking down in sobs.

'I'll be right there,' she said.

The doctor checked on me one last time and revealed the horrible truth – the only reason why I still had my eyes was because I was conscious when Shane was pressing his thumbs into them.

'You instinctively screwed up your eyes, which protected them. It's near impossible for someone to gouge your eyes out for the force that they would need to use,' he tried to reassure me.

I felt sick.

Moments later, Mum and my older sister Tracey pulled back the curtain.

'Oh my God,' Mum shrieked, covering her mouth with her hand. They both burst into tears.

'Look what he's done to you,' Mum cried, grabbing hold of

my hand. She bowed her head onto me. 'That evil bastard,' she
sobbed, shaking her bleached-blonde hair from side to side.
Lorraine must have told her about Shane.

'All right, Trace?' I said to my sister, who was a year older,
and had turned a ghostly shade of white. She was so upset she
couldn't speak. I hated seeing my family crying over me, it
made me feel sick. I was actually going to be sick.

'Nurse, can I please have a sick pan?' I asked, clutching my
hand over my mouth to hold down the vomit.

My sick was black. I vomited again, and again, I couldn't
stop.

'Oh, Tina,' Mum whimpered, stroking my back. 'My poor
girl.'

We had to keep stopping for me to throw up as Mum drove
me home and the black vomit kept coming. My body had gone
into shock, and I must have been sick at least sixty times in the
next twenty-four hours.

I had just finished crouching over the toilet for the umpteenth
time when my mobile rang. It was an unknown caller, so I
answered, thinking it was the police. They had already told me
Shane had pleaded not guilty to the charges and had been bailed
with a restraining order not to contact me, and I thought they
might be updating me.

It was Shane. I was going to be sick again.

7
Fresh Start

I thought the police were pulling my house apart from the drilling noises that were coming from my bedroom. Workmen stomped up and down my stairs carrying tools, as I stood in the hallway feeling like a spare part.

'Mind out,' they said as they brought through my new bedroom door.

I'd never seen such a thick piece of wood in my life. Not even an elephant would be able to get through that. I sighed with relief. The copper called me up when the refurbishments were installed.

'This is your panic room,' he announced. It was going to be my bolt hole if Shane came after me again.

'You lock it like this,' he said.

I jumped at the sound of the bolts sliding across.

'One, two and three,' he showed me. And then he handed me a panic alarm on a rope which I could wear around my neck.

'Press this and we will know where you are in the house,' he illustrated.

But what if Shane locks me in the panic room? I kept my thoughts to myself though. I knew Shane wouldn't come near me again. He was meant to appear in court at the start of that month for beating me up, and he wouldn't dare break his bail conditions.

He tried to weave his way around them though. For the next few days, Shane got his friends to ring me and they would quickly pass him the phone. 'Leave me alone,' I'd shout down the receiver. Just the sound of his voice made me shake, as it sent a river of flashbacks running through me.

'No, Shane, no,' I remembered screaming, as he towered over me. I couldn't forget the image of his thumbs digging into my eyes. Paul was taking care of the kids while I recovered, so I went to stay with Lorraine to get some peace, some support.

'Don't you dare take him back,' my sister barked, when I told her Shane had been trying to get in contact. 'You hear me,' she said, pointing her finger.

'Of course, what do you take me for?' I beat her off. How could she think I would take him back?

'You can do so much better, Tine,' she said, softening, pulling me in for a hug.

I nodded, but inside I didn't believe it. By beating me up, Shane had made me feel worthless. I felt like a piece of shit.

'You can do better, Tina,' I said to myself in Lorraine's bathroom mirror.

'Can you?' I questioned, as I stared at my disgusting reflection. My face had now turned from black to purple and yellow. Miraculously no bones were broken, but my eyes were so black and swollen I looked like a freaky insect. My hair was greasy and scraped back in a tight knot.

'You look old and ugly. He's laughing at you, he's laughing because he knows no one is going to want you.' Tears filled my punched eyes.

I lifted my aching hands up to my face only to reveal a whole load more bruises. Thinking Shane may have cheated on me hurt more than my beating because it made me feel even more worthless. I touched the taps to splash water on my face and a pain rocketed through my thumbs.

'Owwww,' I screamed, and my knees buckled, sending me to the floor.

'What, what?' quizzed Lorraine as she rushed in to find me hugging my thumbs.

'I felt them click back into place,' I sobbed, tears of pain streaming from my eyes. 'I knew they were dislocated.'

'Oh, Tine,' Lorraine said, scooping me off the lino floor. Her eyes were filled with pity, which I hated to see. I didn't want anyone's pity.

'It's OK to be upset,' she whispered, tucking the loose strands of my hair behind my ear.

I bit my lip to stop myself crying again. I wrapped my arms around her neck and she hugged me tightly just like we used to do when we were kids. We used to all huddle together on the same bed because we couldn't bear being apart. I needed my sisters more than ever now.

I was going to need their support when I came face to face with Shane tomorrow. The police had arranged to chaperone him while he picked up his things from my house – the things he'd left in the street the night he was arrested. That night I dreamed of Shane picking me up and throwing me down my stairs, scooping me up and chucking me, again, and again.

I expected two cops at the most to watch over Shane, but there must have been at least ten in my house the following day, with riot vans parked outside in my street. God, they must think he's a dangerous monster if I need all this protection, I thought.

'He's here,' one of the officers warned, as he was brought up in a van.

'You going to be OK?' he asked, as I heard the van door slide open.

'Yep.' I nodded defiantly. But I felt that sick feeling rise in my gut. I ran to the downstairs loo and vomited with nerves. How can one person make you feel this way? I wondered. I coughed and spluttered, splashed water on my face and walked back out to face the music.

Shane was swaggering up my path flanked by police officers. He strutted like he was ten men; swaggering in the same way as he walked around Penzance. Even though I was trembling inside I crossed my arms at the door to show him who was boss. He glared at me and then smirked.

'Admiring your handiwork?' I said sarcastically.

'Ha!' He tossed his head back and stomped into my front room.

The commotion had attracted an audience, as half the street were now hanging out of their windows or sitting on their walls to watch Shane remove his things. First to go were his box of DVDs. He heaved them into his arms and carried them out but the bottom of the box broke and his horror films scattered across my front garden.

My neighbours roared with laughter.

He snarled and then scooped them up into his arms. I could tell that hurt his massive ego. He came back and forth at least fifteen times and I was there watching his every move with my arms crossed like a bouncer. You bastard, I thought, as I got a whiff of his familiar Lynx deodorant, which I associated with our love-making. I loved you and you broke us.

I was just about to close the door on him when he turned around and asked for the one thing I had hidden from him – his testosterone boosters.

'Where's my M1Ts?' he said, charging forward.

'Ease up!' A copper held out an arm to barricade him out.

'No, it's fine, if he wants his pills he can have them,' I scoffed. I pulled the jar from out of the kitchen cupboard and slapped them into his palm. They were partly to blame, as far as I was concerned, as his anger had got worse since he started popping them.

The cops escorted him to the end of my garden and then he pulled out a beer can and lifted it in the air.

'Wha-hey,' he sang and took a glug.

'Go home,' I shouted, and turned my back on him. The police officers closed in and I heard them telling him to move on. As soon as I closed my door I sank back against the wall with relief. It had taken every last ounce of strength to keep me standing through that, because as much as I hated him, seeing Shane again brought all those intense feelings of love back.

They say there is a thin line between love and hate and I could feel that now. And I hated myself for feeling it. The trouble with Shane was he knew exactly what buttons to press to get my attention. He couldn't reach me by phone so he decided to make me jealous instead.

'Oh my God, Tine, I've just seen Shane leave the house down the street,' Lorraine gasped as she chatted on the phone.

'You're joking me, what's he doing on your estate?' I asked.

We didn't have to wait long for an answer, though. Shane sent a message to my sister via Facebook explaining his new-found interest along the road.

'Don't worry, I won't be bothering your sister, I've got a new girlfriend called Anne,' he boasted.

'He's doing this to wind me up!' I screamed in anger when Lorraine showed me the entry.

'Well, it's working,' Lorraine said, closing down her webpage.

'He's deliberately chosen her to rub it in my face. Idiot,' I fumed, dismissing him.

The trouble was Lorraine was right, his game was working. Thinking about him having sex with her made me feel even more low. There I was, covered in bruises, stuck at home with the kids while he was having a whale of a time.

'I'll tell him to leave us alone,' Lorraine said. 'Don't take any notice of him, Tina,' she ordered, looking right at me. I nodded but the doubts were already starting to creep in. I dreamed of walking in on him having sex with Anne in my bed. I opened the door and he was there, working away on her.

'Shane,' I shouted. He turned his head and smirked.

'Get out of my house,' I ordered. He ignored me.

'Get out!' I screamed. He just carried on having sex as if I was invisible.

I woke up dripping. I wiped the sweat from my bruised arms and was reminded who I'd become – the battered ugly ex-girlfriend. I couldn't get the image of them out of my head.

Maybe it was my fault that he got so angry? It had to be. He wasn't like that normally, so it must be down to me. I'd started to feel delirious through my lack of sleep.

I had to pull it together for the sake of my children, though, especially as Shane's attack had led to social services knocking on my door. As soon as I told them I wasn't with Shane any more they closed the case and left me to recover, but that didn't stop me worrying about how that night had left a mark on my poor boys. The painful sound of Liam crying echoed around my mind. I thought about Ben's terrified face every day. Ben didn't want to talk to me about what he saw but I could tell he was frightened for his mummy, because he wouldn't leave my side. He kept wanting to help me in any way he could by making me cups of tea and asking me if I needed him.

Shane had been like a dad to my boys over the past six months, which made everything hurt so much more. I thought I'd finally found a husband in Shane and I was struggling to cope with the bubble bursting. I was torn between thinking I was the idiot for being blinded by his charm, to blaming myself for bringing out the worst in him. When you start to feel like you're on the scrapheap you lower your standards because you feel you don't deserve better. Maybe this was the best I could get – a partner who was Jekyll and Hyde – and I should just shut up and put up with it?

The less sleep I got, the more my thoughts would spiral. Shane was messaging Lorraine every day so I still felt like I was in his clutches. I didn't have space to breathe and I was so anxious, I didn't feel like eating. My tiny frame was shrinking by the day and Tracey stopped by to have a word.

'I've seen birds eat more than you,' she scolded, as I picked at the biscuit with my cup of tea. 'We're worried about you, Tine,' she said, squeezing my arm. Although Tracey was only a year older than me she had adopted the mothering role in the family. We shared a room growing up and she used to let me climb into her bed when I couldn't sleep. Mum hated us smoking but Trace always kept a lookout for Mum coming up the stairs, while I was hanging out the window puffing away. Trace has always been my rock, the sensible one who I could depend on. I'd confided in Lorraine about Shane up until now because I knew Tracey would be disapproving and I didn't want to hear it.

'I'll make you another cup of tea but only if you eat the sandwich I've made for you,' she blackmailed.

'All right, girl,' I lied.

She sat down next to me and shook her head as she looked at my battered and bruised body. I could see her eyes welling up and I tried to switch the mood.

'I'm going to be OK,' I said, putting up my wall of steel.

'Have you heard from him?' she asked, concerned.

I told her Shane had been emailing Lorraine every night trying to get a message to me.

'One minute he's writing he loves me, that he misses me, that he wants me back. The next he's saying I'm a bitch. I don't understand it, Trace, he's the one who's met someone else. Why is he being nice then nasty?' Talking about Shane suddenly made me anxious, a feeling that was constantly simmering underneath my bruised skin.

'Has he said sorry?' She asked the most obvious of questions. I couldn't believe it. I was so in shock I hadn't even stopped to ask myself that.

'No,' I said in disbelief.

Tracey cringed with disgust. She leaned forward to scold me some more.

'Don't you dare take him back. If you take him back the family will disown you,' she warned. She knew my family meant more to me than anything.

'I won't, Trace, I won't,' I promised.

Her words were the wake-up call I needed. I told Lorraine to email Shane with a venomous message: 'Leave my sister alone. You've got a girlfriend now so stop bothering her. You obviously didn't give a shit about her because you beat her up.'

I signed up to a dating website to help me believe I could do better than Shane, that there were plenty more fish out there. I posted a picture of me laughing, the Tina before the bruises. I couldn't believe how quickly I got a response – from a DJ who ran parties on a boat. Dan was mixed-race, shaven-headed, chiselled jaw, hot body – from his photos he looked like a better-looking version of Shane.

We chatted on email about our mutual love of DJ-ing, about clubbing, surfing. I loved the attention and the fact he was so keen to meet me.

'He's invited me to come as a VIP guest to his boat party this weekend,' I boasted to Lorraine.

'Let's do it,' she squealed, keen to get out of Penzance for a night.

I told Dan we would be there but, as Saturday night approached, I started to get cold feet. It had been nearly four weeks since the attack but the bruises were still visible like a tattoo, forever reminding me of that night. I did a test run, applying my make-up to see if I could hide the damage. I carefully rubbed the foundation over my yellow-stained cheeks, followed by powder, and then bronzer and then blusher. I could still see the bruised glow showing through.

'This is never going to work,' I wailed, slamming my make-up into the sink basin.

'No matter what you do, you're still going to look old and ugly,' I told my reflection. I looked more like a transvestite with all the make-up I'd trowelled onto my skin. I was a joke. I called up Lorraine and broke the bad news to her.

'I just don't feel in the mood,' I told her, trying to let her down gently. The truth was I was scared I wasn't good enough for Dan; that he would take one look at me and tell me I wasn't his cup of tea. I wrote him an email at the eleventh hour saying I wasn't feeling very well.

'Poor you, come next Saturday instead,' he chirped. He was keen all right; I just had to believe in myself more.

I hadn't seen Shane for five weeks and my self-esteem was finally picking up thanks to Dan chasing me and making me feel wanted. I'd stopped crying in bed at night and I was putting my energy into decorating the living room. Shane had lost his grip on me and I had returned to the Tina that everyone knew and loved. The Tina that didn't take any crap from men. The Tina that was going to meet Dan at the weekend and show off her DJ skills.

I was rummaging through my wardrobe looking for what I could wear to the party the next day when my mobile rang. It was a Penzance number so I picked up.

'Don't hang up, T.'

It was him.

I felt like someone had punched me in the stomach. I couldn't speak.

'I love you and I miss you,' he went on.

I was going to be sick.

'What have you been up to? I've missed you,' he said, forcing me to reply.

'Just taking care of myself. Getting on with it,' I said, trying to sound cool and detached when my heart was thumping out of my chest.

I heard him breathing down the other end of the line as he thought what to say next.

'I can't get you out of my head.' Pang! Another arrow to my heart. These were the things I'd been longing to hear for five weeks, for me to know he didn't really think I was as worthless as he had treated me. His voice was calm and sad; he was the teddy-bear Shane again who I'd loved.

'I've been so upset,' he went on, drilling deeper into my emotions.

'I've been really upset as well,' I interrupted. 'I was so gutted about what you did,' I said, putting my head into my hands.

He quickly changed the subject, pretending like that night had never happened.

'I want to come and see you,' he mumbled. I could imagine him hugging the phone, wishing he was hugging me.

'No, you can't come and see me. I'll get in trouble with the police,' I snapped. What an idiot for wanting to break his bail conditions – always wanting to be the outlaw. We must have chatted for half an hour before I rang off, feeling more confused than ever. Damn it, I'd done all this work on myself and he had reeled me back in again.

'I HATE YOU, SHANE!' I screamed, flinging my mobile across the room. The truth was, I didn't hate him at all, I loved him.

I couldn't sleep a wink that night. I kept getting up and checking on the boys and then going downstairs to drink another glass of water. My stomach was so empty it felt like it was eating itself. I liked the attention I was getting from Shane, knowing he had chosen me over young Anne, but I couldn't forget what he had done. At least Lorraine was coming around my place in the morning – she'd sort my head out.

I had just got up and was making myself a brew when my phone bleeped. One phone conversation with Shane and I was back to jumping at every noise. I checked my text message – 'I'm coming around yours now'. Shane was on his way over, what was I going to do? I put my hands over my eyes like I used to do when I was scared as a child.

My hands were trembling so much I could barely write a reply: 'no don't come over I'm going out'. He wouldn't come now, I was sure of it. Seconds later Lorraine pulled up outside with some clothes she thought I might like for the boat party that night. I must have had fear and panic written over my face.

'What's up, Tine?' she frowned.

It all happened so quickly, I had no time to explain.

Lorraine looked out the kitchen window and squealed, 'Shane's outside!'

I jumped a foot in the air. It had been nearly five weeks since I had last seen him and I'd forgotten how enormous he was. He was wearing his Cornish Pirates rugby jersey and he still had his man-about-town swagger.

'I told him not to turn up,' I hissed.

'What? You spoke to him?' Lorraine demanded.

'Yeah, I spoke to him last night,' I confessed, and hung my head with shame.

Lorraine was furious that I had gone against all her advice. 'I can't believe you spoke to him,' she snapped. She didn't want me to answer the door but I was panicking – I was scared of Shane, scared the police would turn up at my house. He looked at me with his puppy eyes and I reached my arm out and grabbed him by the scruff.

'Just get in,' I said, yanking him into my kitchen. My adrenalin was going, so I wasn't thinking straight.

Lorraine curled up her lips into her mouth. She didn't say a word, she just glared at Shane like she hated every inch of him. She shook her head as if to say she couldn't believe he was there.

'I didn't know he was going to turn up,' I mouthed.

I could smell his Lynx deodorant and then I got a whiff of booze. He smelled like he had slept in a brewery. He lurched forward and tried to kiss me. The arrogance of it! I pushed him off and crossed my arms to keep him away. I wasn't comfortable with him touching me – the last time had been to pick me up and chuck me down my stairs.

He came forward again and I turned on my side to block his advance. He was so big and overbearing that I knew now he was in my house I wouldn't be able to get rid of him. He went for me again, this time trying to lock me into a cuddle.

'No,' I hissed, pushing him away. But my body was now craving his touch.

Fight it, fight the feeling.

'I've missed you, T,' he grovelled. 'I've been so low, I haven't been able to stop thinking about you.'

'I can't bear to watch this,' Lorraine snapped. 'Are you going to be OK?' she had to ask.

I nodded. I felt so guilty for letting her down, but I now felt like I was piggy in the middle.

After Lorraine had left he carried on. 'I love you,' he insisted. He might as well have been on his hands and knees.

I shook my head in turmoil. 'I can't get my head around what you did to me,' I said. Shane did his best to keep me talking but about everything except the attack.

'I'm going to sort my life out, T,' he promised. 'I'm going to get a job and I'm going to get back into my rugby.'

'You better had, because I'm not having you watching TV here all day again,' I threatened.

'I promise, T,' he grovelled. 'And I'll have my own house soon. I've moved into a pass house around the corner from my old place, so I'm now on the council-house waiting list. It's like a halfway house but the people living there are all right, you know.'

'And what happened between you and Kate that night?' I pushed for the truth.

Shane looked me straight in the eye: 'I never touched her. She threw herself at me, but I told her I wasn't interested.' He sounded so sincere it was hard not to believe him.

'OK,' I nodded.

After several hours in my house he had dug a tunnel back under my skin because he'd reminded me of our love, how much I'd missed him.

He followed me everywhere like a puppy, even into the bathroom, as I went to splash water on my face. I turned around and he was sitting there on the bath, blocking my exit – there was no escape. He grabbed my waist and pulled me into him. My skin tingled with his touch. He cupped my face in his hands and kissed me gently like I was the most precious thing on earth.

'I miss you and I love you,' he whispered between kisses.

I let myself melt into his arms.

That night we made love. It was slow and gentle, a far cry from the monster I'd seen five weeks ago. He fell asleep with his big bear arms hugging me into his chest while I cried silent tears.

One more week and I would have been over him, I cried. I was supposed to meet Dan tonight but Shane got there first. It felt so good to have Shane back but I also felt sick with guilt.

I'd made my bed so now I was going to have to lie in it.

8

The Girl Who Cried Wolf

Shane knocked on the wall between my bedroom and my kids' room.

'What was the point of them putting in a panic room? I could come through this wall instead. I'd be there in seconds,' he gloated.

'What do you mean?' I asked nervously, as he destroyed my confidence in the one place I felt safe.

'I could run through this,' he laughed.

I imagined him charging through my wall like a rhino while I cowered in the corner. He was right; there was no place he wouldn't be able to get to me. I shivered.

'You'd better go home. I can't risk the police catching you here.' I changed the subject. 'I don't want social services questioning me again. It's better if I come and see you in Penzance.'

He shrugged, as if to say he couldn't give a damn if the police caught him.

'What they going to do if they catch me?' he sniffed. He was clearly in one of his moods where he thought he could take on the world.

'What about my kids?' I asked.

'They want to punish me, not you, stop worrying.'

Shane rode his bike home and I made my way down to Nan's for a cup of tea and a hug. I needed to tell someone about Shane pushing his way back into my life and Nan was the only person who would hear me out. I was too late – Lorraine had got there first.

'Don't come crying down here to us when he beats you up again,' Uncle Glen growled as he let me in.

'He forced his way in, what choice did I have?' I tried to defend myself.

'You make your bed, you lie in it,' he said with a look of disgust. Hearing those words actually spoken sent a shiver down my spine, like a premonition of my impending doom.

'Take no notice of him, love,' Nan said, beckoning me over to the table where she had a cup of tea and cake ready for me. For the first time in years I felt uncomfortable around my family, like I was an outcast.

I shyly picked at my coconut cake. My stomach was too knotted to eat.

'Uncle Glen just worries about you, dear. We all do,' Nan told me with a smile. I felt sick with guilt. Nan was like a mum to me and I felt like I'd let her down the most.

I bet she thinks what a waste of space I am after all those years she put into raising me? I thought to myself. And she'd be right. I am a complete mug.

'I know, Nan,' I said, trying to change the conversation. I don't know how she did it – she managed to keep a smile on her face come rain or shine. I wished I could be as strong as her. She wouldn't have let passion rule her heart; Nan would have given Shane his marching orders months ago. I decided I would be better off keeping my distance from now on so she wouldn't worry about me and I wouldn't feel guilty for going against all her worldly advice.

'Your mum says she's taking you and the girls for supper this week,' Nan went on.

I was dreading sitting around a table with them all giving me the third degree.

'Yeah. That'll be lovely,' I lied. I wondered which one of them would be the most scathing. Why was I getting angry at them? They had every right to be upset with me. My guilt was clearly eating me up.

I nearly pulled out of our pub dinner as I guess I wasn't ready to face the truth. I told them I wasn't coming and then at the last minute showed up down the road. Their faces said a thousand words – you could tell they were all related by the similar frown that was etched across their foreheads.

'All right, Tine?' Lorraine broke the ice. Mum and Tracey avoided eye contact by burying their heads in the menu.

'Yeah,' I replied shyly. I squeezed along the bench and tried to fit in.

They talked about what to have from the meal deal, about Tracey's kids, about anything except Shane. It was like he was the elephant in the room that everyone was pretending not to see. My phone rang and my heart sank – now was not the time.

'Hi . . . What? . . . You're coming over now? OK.' I hung up. Tracey glared at me with sad eyes.

'Was that Shane?' She almost choked on his name.

'Yeah,' I mumbled. I felt like I was in school being told off.

'I've got to meet him at the bus stop,' I explained.

Tracey and Mum rolled their eyes.

'What the hell are you doing?' asked Tracey. 'He's breaking his bail conditions, what will the police do when they find out?'

I shrugged, as I knew I was sticking my head in the sand.

'Don't bother bringing him back here because none of us want to see his face,' she carried on. I thought she was going to cry she was so distressed. I tried to calm the situation but then the storm hit.

'Shane's here,' Tracey said, pointing behind me.

My heart lurched as he caught me off guard again. I was turning into a nervous wreck. I spun around and Shane was strolling across the pub like he owned the place. He said hello to some people he knew and then came up to our table. You'd think he would be wary facing my family, but no, he acted like they should be grateful he had stopped by. He leaned forward to give me a kiss and I squirmed in my seat. I could feel all my family's eyes on me. He held out his hand and introduced himself to my mum. She kept her arms firmly crossed and he was left hanging.

'I'll take a seat, then,' he said, brushing it off. Shane pulled up a pew next to Mum, which left Tracey and Lorraine free to give me a hard time. We were so busy bickering I hadn't noticed how Mum and Shane were getting on like a house on fire. I stared in disbelief as she threw back her bleached-blonde hair with laughter. She looked at me and shrugged an expression as if to say, 'He's not as bad as I thought he'd be.'

Shane had her eating out of his palm. He smugly winked at me, acknowledging his handiwork. That was the thing with him: he could be Prince Charming when he wanted to be. Shane could be so convincing he would make you believe something was white when it was actually black.

I couldn't get him to leave the table, he was having so much fun holding court. I was pleased he was getting on with Mum but it made me feel even more afraid of him – he was more powerful and convincing than I first realised. We finally made our excuses and headed back to my house.

'I think I was a hit,' he boasted as we strolled along.

'I can't go through that ever again. My sisters hate me. I'm going to stay clear of them for a while,' I muttered.

'What?' Shane wasn't listening; he was too busy basking in his latest victory.

'I reckon I could talk my way out of anything, you know,' he went on. I rolled my eyes with irritation. I was tearing my family apart and he was talking about himself.

'So talk your way out of what you did to me, then,' I snapped. I wanted answers and I still didn't have any. 'Why, Shane? Why did you do it?' I couldn't let it go.

'What? What do you want me to say?' he asked, shrugging dismissively.

'Tell me why you hit me,' I demanded.

He shrugged again and carried on walking.

'Why?'

He ignored me.

I could forgive but I couldn't forget, and the more he ignored me the more it ate me up inside. I let it drop for the moment but the memories reared their ugly head again while we were watching a DVD. As usual, it was his choice of film, and he decided to stick on *28 Days Later* – a horror film about how a virus has turned everyone in London into killers.

I could barely look at the screen, so I nuzzled my head into his big chest and breathed in his manly smell. It was so good to be back in his arms and I was already allowing him to call the shots. He stroked my arms and my skin tingled. I stroked his hand and I couldn't wait for the horrid film to be over so we could go to bed.

Shane jumped to the edge of the sofa with excitement.

'What?' I asked, as I fell back onto the sofa.

'Check this out,' he sniggered, rewinding the disc.

I watched in horror as he played back the scene in slow motion.

'Oh my God,' I retched, as a woman strapped down to a hospital bed gets punched in the face several times by her crazy husband. She's screaming and begging for her life as he sticks his thumbs into her eyes; blood is squirting everywhere.

'Turn it off!' I screamed.

He burst out laughing.

'Now,' I cried, my hands still protecting my eyes. Was this some kind of sick joke?

'It's just a film,' he said, wrapping his arms around me. 'Come on, T.' He tried to fob it off but I felt sick in the pit of my stomach; a grinding, gnawing pain at the memory of him pushing and turning his thumbs. My hands trembled uncontrollably.

Shane pulled my face to his and kissed me gently, which helped me relax. I was like a puppet on strings where he was controlling how I felt. One minute I was terrified, the next I was feeling protected and loved. He picked up the controller and pressed play again. I just had to grin and bear it.

I quietly cried myself to sleep that night. The film had left me shaky and I couldn't calm myself down. I rolled over to look at Shane and my heart sank. I love you, I thought, but I'm such a mug for loving you. Another tear rolled down my cheek and bled into the pillow.

I woke up needing answers again. It was the only way I could move on if I could understand why Shane had beaten the crap out of me. If I knew why, I might be able to understand. If it was something I'd done then I could work on not upsetting him again like that. I shook my head with disbelief – what are you saying, Tina, that you may have been to blame, snap out of it. I was having conversations with myself, I felt so confused.

'Shane, why did you do this to me?' I tentatively asked, as he played computer games.

He looked up as if to say, 'What now?'

'Come on, Shane, you owe me an explanation.' I forced the words out.

'I didn't do it,' he said and stared.

What? Was I hearing this?

'What do you mean you didn't do it?'

'It's all in your head,' he said, firing his controller stick at the screen.

I couldn't believe he was taking the piss out of me. I planted my hands onto my hips to control my shaky fingers.

'Why are you lying?' I felt so confused.

'You're making it up,' he chuckled.

'I was in the bloody room, I know exactly what happened, Shane,' I shouted.

He blanked me.

'Shane, what the hell?'

No answer.

I flung my arms up in the air and walked into the garden to cool off. He was making me feel like I was going nuts. How could he say I made it up? Did he actually believe his own lies, or was he just playing with me? My heart was hammering – I was angry and scared and confused all at the same time.

The more he taunted me, the more I hassled him for answers.

He cut me dead the next time with, 'Stop making a mountain out of a molehill.'

He was making me wonder whether I was turning the attack into something worse than it actually was. I didn't break any bones, after all. It was an argument that just got out of hand; it happens in lots of relationships, I reasoned. But I wanted an apology. That was the very least I deserved. Wasn't it?

'I want you to say sorry,' I started again, after we had been bickering.

'What?' he said, stepping out of my downstairs bathroom.

'You owe me an apology,' I insisted.

He raised his hands to the sky and spun on his heels like he was performing for a hidden audience.

'Is this a set-up? Are there cameras filming me?' he joked. I glared at him as he cackled with laughter.

'Are you for real?' I asked in disbelief. He clutched his belly he was laughing so hard. 'This ain't funny, Shane, you really hurt me.' But it was falling on deaf ears.

I turned my back on him and walked away from the argument.

And just like that his laughter stopped and I felt his big arm grab me from behind and lock my neck in his elbow.

'Stop,' I gargled, trying to tear at his arm with my hands. It was like having a killer python wrapped around my neck.

He released his hold without saying a word and I coughed for air. I should have known better than think he was letting me go as, a second later, he grabbed hold again and squeezed ten times as hard. The room got darker and then faded to black.

The next thing I heard was the sound of my breathing – short and shallow, like I was on the edge of death. Then I felt something wet blowing hard on my lips and a man calling my name.

'I'm sorry, Tina, please wake up.'

A shooting pain bolted through my neck.

'Please wake up, I love you,' the voice pleaded.

Just opening my eyes was exhausting. I blinked my eyelids apart and saw Shane bowing over me, about to give me mouth-to-mouth resuscitation. Sheer panic was etched across his face.

'You're alive,' he spluttered.

I couldn't speak for the pain and shock. The last thing I remember was being outside the bathroom but this didn't look like my hallway. There was a bookshelf and a chest of drawers and a pile of clothes that all looked a lot like mine. I was in my bedroom – how did I get here? Shane curled up next to me on my mattress and wouldn't take his eyes off me.

'I thought I'd killed you,' he whispered. 'I've never seen anyone take so long to come around from a sleeper hold,' he said, stroking my limp hand. 'You were out cold for twenty minutes.' He kept stroking.

I was too weary to reply. I lay there like a broken toy that had been thrown around a room. I stared at the light from the street trying to pass through my curtains until my eyelids got so heavy they let me fall asleep.

I woke up in more pain than when I had gone to bed. Remembering everything in the morning was one of the worst feelings in the world. Luckily it was Sunday and the boys were still with Paul. The thought of them seeing me in a state again was too much to stomach.

Shane wasn't speaking; he was just lying on his side watching me. I slid to the edge of the bed and tried to stand up but my legs crumpled beneath me like a newborn foal. I tried again but my knees buckled and I crashed to the carpet. I could feel Shane's eyes examining my every painful move, but still he never said a word. I had no choice but to crawl on my hands and knees to the door. I reached up my arm but he'd locked the bolts. Shane had locked us into my panic room – the one place that was supposed to keep him out.

'I need the toilet, where's the keys?' I begged.

He stared with his stony eyes and then rolled over and pulled out a key from under him. He stretched out his arm, making me crawl to collect it. I felt so humiliated as I pulled myself across the mattress, every ounce of dignity gone.

I used the door frame to help me to my feet and then staggered into the bathroom, collapsing on the toilet seat. 'It will be OK, it will be OK,' I repeated. I felt delirious with the pain and didn't know whether to laugh or cry. I caught a glimpse of the necklace of bruises around my throat as I staggered past the mirror. How was I going to hide this?

I slowly made my way downstairs, step by step, and then carefully lay down on the sofa, pulling Liam's Thomas the Tank Engine quilt over me. I felt like all the life had been sucked out of me, like an old lady on her death bed.

Please, God, I'll never mention another word about the attack — again I pleaded for the pain to go away.

Shane followed me and sat legs-apart on the sofa opposite, watching my every breath. I couldn't bear to look at him I was so angry. I couldn't bring myself to speak. I was too scared he would do it again. For several hours we lay there in silence, as I played over the horror of the night before in my head. Shane finally spoke, to pin the blame on me.

'It's all your fault,' he stabbed. 'If you hadn't kept going on at me this never would have happened.'

I kept my mouth shut this time. There was no way I was going to answer back. And maybe he was right? I probably did make a mountain out of a molehill. I was too weak to fight his reasoning. One thing was for sure, I wasn't going to tell anyone about this. I could hear it now — 'I told you so'. I was better off keeping it a secret and dealing with the painful times on my own. And I couldn't risk upsetting Shane because he wouldn't like it if I was blabbing to my family about what he had done. What if he started punishing my sisters for my mistakes?

Keeping my mouth shut worked — things were back to normal by that evening. I threw on a smile for Shane and when I couldn't take the charade any longer I quietly made my way to the bathroom, locked the door and drowned my tears in a bath full of water.

'How has it come to this?' I sobbed to myself, splashing water over my bruised, skinny body.

I knew there was no getting away now.

9

Under the Thumb

'Write it again,' Shane ordered as he loomed over my shoulder. 'I'm going to end up in prison if you don't get this letter to the police right.' He was trying to guilt-trip me.

I screwed up the paper and poised my pen for the fifth time, as I waited for him to dictate how I wanted to drop the GBH charges against him. I was scared if I didn't lie to the police he'd beat me up again. He'd turned it round to make me feel guilty that I'd had him arrested in April. He tugged on my heartstrings and made me feel sorry for him.

'You're the only person I have left,' he'd said as he poured his heart out the night before. 'I don't have any real friends. My mum and dad couldn't give a shit about me, my dad's even disowned me since he found out about what happened to you in April,' he whimpered.

How could I throw him away when everyone else had? He stood in my kitchen like a little boy lost who needed my help.

'I was put into care when I was fourteen.' He winced at the memory.

This was the first time Shane had opened up in the ten months I'd known him.

'My parents had left me on my own in their house to fend for myself while Dad went off to the Marines and Mum disappeared to stay with my sister. There was no food or electric, I had nothing and I didn't know what to do.' He stuttered with the painful memory. 'So one night I couldn't survive any longer without food. I grabbed my penknife and robbed someone in the street,' he admitted. His eyes were wide as he relived the moment.

'Oh God, Shane,' I said, reaching out for his hand.

'But the police caught me, and when they found out why I done it they put me into care.' He looked up. He wasn't crying but I could see there was a reservoir building behind his eyes.

'I had no choice. I learned I had to fight to survive,' he explained.

I suddenly understood why he was so violent and I felt deeply sorry for him.

'I'm so sorry for you. I never realised,' I said, hugging him. I felt like he was my child and I had to protect him. I couldn't imagine my poor son Ben going through that.

He broke away to take a slug from his beer can.

'There's more,' he said, stony-faced. 'I used to dig up graves for money.'

'What? You are joking?' I was worried what he was going to pull out of Pandora's Box next.

'Yeah, I used to dig up old graves in the middle of the night looking for antique jewellery.'

I was speechless.

'I was so desperate, you gotta understand,' he reasoned.

It was the sort of thing you hear in crime novels, not from your boyfriend. I can't let him go to prison in this state, I thought. I'd never forgive myself if something happened to him, inside. He'd been badgering me to retract my statement, so I should do it. As soon as I told Shane I'd do it, he pushed a pen and paper under my nose and the bully in him came out again.

'I'm going to tell you what I want you to write,' he ordered.

'OK,' I mumbled.

'Write after me,' he instructed as he paced back and forth across my kitchen. 'I'd like to take back the charges against Shane Jenkin because I lied in my original statement,' he dictated.

My hand froze – I couldn't bring myself to write these lies.

'Do it!' he shouted.

He went on: 'It was me who actually beat Shane up because I was jealous.'

'Jealous?' I shrieked. 'What of exactly?'

'Because you thought I'd slept with Kate,' he said matter-of-factly. 'Now look what you've done, you've ruined my train of thought. Start again,' he ordered, tearing off a new piece of paper.

'We need to say you were swinging at me and then you fell down the stairs because you were drunk,' he said. 'Yeah, yeah, that's it.' He was buzzing from making up lies. 'Actually, second thoughts, scrap that. You need to do it again.' He reached over my shoulder and screwed up my paper.

'OK, I've got it now. You told me to move my things out and you accidentally tripped over some of my stuff and fell down the stairs. That's it,' he said, clapping his hands with glee.

'I feel like such an idiot writing this,' I moaned.

'Just bloody write it,' he ordered. 'You got me in this mess, you get me out of it.'

I nodded obediently and started the letter again on a fresh sheet of paper. The whole process had been so exhausting I just wanted to catch my breath for a moment after I'd finished.

'Well, get on down to the cop shop, then,' he snapped.

I reluctantly pulled myself to my feet and made my way to the bottom of the road to Hayle police station.

'All right?' I sheepishly greeted the copper in reception.

'Hi, Tina,' he said. Everyone knows everyone in these parts and I'd got quite a name for myself after the attack in April. I didn't want to step forward. I had to physically lift my legs. They felt heavy as lead. I took a deep breath and handed over the piece of paper.

'What's this?' he said, examining the folded note.

'I want to retract the charges against Shane Jenkin.' My voice trembled.

'Wait here,' the cop ordered, as he went out the back to grab a more senior officer.

I was led into an interview room where a tubby middle-aged man with cropped hair to mask his balding head sat me down at a table. He had a tired look about him, like he'd heard many a story.

'I hear you want to retract your charges against Shane Jenkin, Miss Nash.'

'Yes, that's correct,' I replied nervously, playing with the fabric of my vest top.

He stared at me as if he knew I was lying. There was an uncomfortable silence for a few minutes as he read through my statement. He shook his head and sighed deeply.

'Well, I'm afraid the damage to you was so severe that we are going to go ahead with the charges anyway because we can do victimless prosecutions.'

'What does that mean?' I asked him in panic.

'It's a new law that has been put in place for cases like yours, Miss Nash, to convict domestic abusers who might otherwise go free as a result of manipulating or threatening their victims to keep them from testifying. We can now convict abusers like Mr Jenkin without the cooperation of the victim.'

'But I'm saying he didn't do it,' I insisted.

Shane's going to kill me, Shane's going to kill me.

'How can you put him away if you don't have my evidence?' Sweat was dripping down my back.

'We can use 999 call recordings and transcripts, child witness statements, neighbour witness statements, paramedic log sheets, prior police reports, restraining orders . . . this list goes on,' he said calmly.

'So there's nothing I can do?' I whimpered.

'No, Miss Nash.' Then he looked me in the eye: 'We're doing this for your own safety.'

I took a big gulp. I was going to get it in the neck now.

I took my time walking back up the road, as I wasn't in a hurry to face the music. A weight had been lifted off my shoulders, as I'd done all I could to help get Shane off, but now there was an even heavier weight, of dread, sitting in my stomach.

'I've been to the station,' I said, forcing a smile as I walked through the door.

'So they're dropping the charges?' Shane walked over.

'There was nothing I could do.' I trembled in his shadow.

'Whad'ya mean?' He glared down at me.

'They're going to carry it on. They said it was such a violent attack they will do it as a victimless prosecution. I told them, Shane, I told them it was my fault,' I stuttered. 'There's nothing I can do.'

I waited for my punishment.

'You haven't done a good enough job. You've got to do better than this.' He clenched his fists. 'Got it?'

I bowed my head and nodded.

I spent the next twenty-four hours panicking about what else I could do to keep Shane out of prison. I couldn't believe only seven weeks ago I wanted him to go down for making a mess of my face and now I was plagued with guilt for thinking I might ruin his life. When I go to his place tonight I'll cook him a nice meal and give him a massage and do my best to make him happy, I thought.

Things didn't go exactly to plan, as Shane went mad at me again for the lack of effort I'd put into trying to clear his name. 'You've got to do better than this,' he kept saying, and went on like a broken record. He didn't stroke my arm or cuddle me when we watched films that night and I was left gasping for his affection.

I barely got a wink of sleep because he kept me up all night concocting a plan of how I was going to save his bacon. I woke up bleary-eyed, exhausted and fed up. I stupidly gave him a mouthful, which fired up his engine. His face went blank and his eyes turned black – I'd seen that look before.

'Go on, I can tell you want to hit me,' I shouted out of desperation.

His face was like stone. I needed to know he would keep his promise to never hit me again.

'Hit me!' I screamed, terrified.

BANG! He punched me in the face.

My skin felt like it had exploded, as I tumbled backwards. I scrambled to my feet and went screaming to his window.

'Help, help!' I shouted to the neighbours.

'Shut up, bitch!' he yelled, as I dodged his approach and sprinted out of his front door and down the street. I clutched my face as I ran, the throbbing pain was already kicking in. Too terrified to turn around, I kept running until I stumbled into some holidaymakers leaving their B&B.

'Are you all right, dear?' one of them asked.

I nodded but kept my head down, fearing my bruises had already taken shape. I looked back – there was no Shane chasing me. The adrenalin was kicking through me so fast it was almost painful. I felt out of control.

What I really wanted to do was cry to my sister but I knew I couldn't go knocking on Lorraine's door for sympathy. Like Uncle Glen said – I'd made my bed, so now I had to lie in it. Also, they wouldn't understand that it was my fault – I provoked him, I deserved it. I anxiously pulled at the skin on my arm with my long, manicured nails, hating myself for being so stupid as to upset Shane. The inferno of pain on my face was quickly subsiding, as my worry for how upset Shane must be took over. He won't forgive you for this, you really upset him this time, I chanted to myself, as I reluctantly made my way home.

By that afternoon I felt sick with guilt. I talked myself into believing I deserved the punch in the face for provoking him. It was a stupid test to see if he would really hit me again and I never should have challenged him. I picked up the phone and dialled Shane.

He answered with a grunt.

'I'm sorry,' I blurted.

He sighed, keeping me on tenterhooks.

'It was my fault. I told you to hit me,' I grovelled.

He sounded impatient, like he was done with me and the hassle I caused him.

'Yeah, it was your fault,' he agreed. 'I'll catch the train over later and we'll sort it out,' he reassured me.

'OK, I'll see you later. I love you.'

But 9 p.m. passed, 10 p.m. passed, 11 p.m. passed and still no Shane. I could hear the train from my bedroom and every time the familiar rumble sounded, I held my breath, hoping he would be on my doorstep minutes later. I lay there waiting and waiting, my stomach knotting with every hour that went past.

Please come, please come, I prayed.

I must have managed to drift off for a while, but I woke up at 5 a.m. feeling sick from having so little food in my stomach. I tried rolling over onto my front to squash the gnawing feeling but there was only one thing that would stop my pain – Shane.

More hours dragged past and he still didn't show. The longer I didn't hear from him the more I blamed myself for him punching me. I'll tell him I'll do anything he wants, I thought. I'll write more letters to the police. Whatever it takes for him to forgive me.

Three more days passed without a word from Shane and I'd cried so much my eyes were more swollen than my battered and bruised cheek. I felt alone and isolated as I couldn't share my grief with my sisters. I tried my best not to show my sorrow to my boys by diving into the bathroom or my bedroom whenever I felt my eyes welling up.

I kept having the worst nightmares – like my subconscious was telling me something different to my heart. I dreamed I had locked myself in my panic room and I'd wrapped my duvet around me to try and protect me.

'Tina, I know you're in there,' Shane taunted from the other side of the door. 'You can't hide from me,' he cooed.

'Leave me alone,' I begged, wrapping the duvet even tighter around my trembling body.

'You know this door can't protect you,' he laughed.

BANG! BANG! BANG! The wall shook as Shane rammed into it.

'Oh God, no.' I pulled the duvet over my face.

BANG! The wall collapsed as Shane charged through from my kids' bedroom. I peeped out from my duvet to see a great big hole in my bedroom, rubble everywhere, and Shane coming for me.

'No, Shane, please,' I begged for my life.

'I told you, you can't keep me out,' he laughed.

'No, Shane!' I woke up screaming in the dead of the night.

My dream was so real I had to check the wall was still there. I got up and looked in on the boys. Ben was fast asleep and I peered into Liam's cot to find his little hand twitching happily from his dream.

'I love you,' I whispered, pulling his quilt up to his smiley face. My boys were the only thing keeping me sane at that moment. If it weren't for them I wouldn't find the will to get out of bed. I was so upset about Shane abandoning me.

I should have known from all the times before that he would eventually show up. He left me on tenterhooks for four days, by which time I'd fallen into the pits of despair.

'You gonna let me in, then?' he said, stinking of booze like he'd been on another one of his benders.

I let him pass through and he stood in my kitchen looking at me, waiting for something.

'I'm sorry, it's my fault,' I admitted, before crumbling into tears.

He watched as I broke down and after he'd seen enough he opened his arms and let me in. I hugged him like I was never going to see him again. His warm body wrapped around me like a blanket, bringing me back to life – the drug addict getting her fix.

'I love you. I'm sorry,' I repeated. 'I'm so sorry.'

10

Honeymoon

When Shane and I weren't fighting it felt so good to be with him that it was like we were on a honeymoon. He'd be cruel and then the old Shane would return to me and we would fall in love all over again. Knowing that honeymoon might be just around the corner helped me put up with the bad stuff.

I tossed the blanket off my sweating body. It was a baking hot Sunday at the end of June and there was no air in Shane's bedroom.

'Come back to bed,' he said, wrapping his strong arms around my tiny waist as I reached over him for the window.

'I need some air,' I giggled, letting him pull me into his chest.

I fended off his advances. 'No, we're not doing it again. It's such a beautiful day, let's go for a walk,' I suggested, wriggling free.

Shane sighed deeply and rolled his naked body over.

'Come on, up,' I insisted.

I threw on my strappy summer dress, scooped my blonde hair into a tight ponytail, and slipped into my flip-flops. It was 11 a.m. by the time we set foot outside Shane's front door and the concrete was already burning hot from the sun. I reached inside my bag and pulled out my favourite sunglasses with diamanté stones on the sides.

'Come on, then,' I said, grabbing his hand and leading him to the supermarket.

It was tourist season and the hilly high street was bustling with holidaymakers darting in and out of the trinket shops. The seagulls were screeching and fighting over empty chip wrappings. I kept my head down so no one would recognise me – I'd kept a low profile since the beating in April and I didn't want it getting back to my sisters that I'd been seen in town with Shane. Tracey and Lorraine knew we were back together but I'd barely seen them since I let Shane back into my life because I felt too guilty being around them.

'Let's just buy the cans and go,' I said, hurrying Shane through the Co-op.

We bought some beers and trundled through the narrow streets to the seafront. There were even more tourists there, walking, cycling, in-line skating along the promenade. I used my hand as a visor and stared out to sea.

'You can see St Michael's Mount from here,' I exclaimed, looking at the picturesque castle on the tiny granite island that could only be reached when the tide was out. I remembered Nan taking us there when we were kids and me scaring the life out of my brother Paul when I jumped out from behind an alcove. I didn't dare ask Shane if he went there when he was young, as I didn't want to bring up any bad memories and ruin our special day.

'Let's climb over the wall and sit on the rocks over there,' I suggested.

'Shane jumped over in one fell swoop and reached his taut, muscled arm down like a vine for me to climb. One yank and I flew up by his side. I was as light as a feather compared with the weights he was used to lifting.

Over the wall, we were away from the main tourist trail, and had the rocks and the sea to ourselves. We scaled across them, their jagged edges spearing through the soles of our flip-flops. We passed white clams hanging on for dear life and crabs scurrying into rock pools to hide from our shadows.

'Wow, look at the view!' I paused with my hands on my hips. 'This is paradise.'

We'd walked far enough, so I set up base on a flat ridge that would make a great dive board.

'I'm going to go swimming,' I announced, peering over the edge.

'Yeah, let's do it,' Shane said with a grin.

We looked at each other as we both thought the same thing – we didn't have any swimmers. Shane shrugged and started undressing anyway, leaving a neat pile of his clothes on the rock.

'Why not?' I blushed. I was a Cornish girl after all. I stripped to my bra and pants and followed Shane down the rocky path to the water's edge. Shane jumped in first and I splashed in after.

'Oh my God,' I squealed. I'd forgotten how cold the English sea was. I trod water as he dived under, pretending to be a shark.

'Get off.' I kicked my legs free from his grip. He rose to the surface, spluttering and laughing.

'Very funny, Shane,' I said, flicking water at him.

He wiped his face and looked up to the scorching sun. The light sparkled as they caught the sea drops in his long dark eyelashes. It was the most perfect romantic moment I could have dreamed of. I'd longed for a moment like this for months and now I had it I didn't want to let go.

I swam towards Shane and wrapped my legs around his big body. He was built like a tank and I could barely get a clasp. He reached his hands onto my bum and pulled me close; there was no escape. Our lips touched and I could taste him and the salty sea as we kissed. I melted from the warmth of the sun on my face, the warmth of his tongue in my mouth. If this isn't heaven, I don't know what is, I thought, smiling inside.

I could feel Shane getting aroused but I wasn't going to go further. I was shy at heart. We stayed in each other's arms kissing for what seemed like forever, until my legs finally gave in with cramp from the cold. Shane pulled me onto the shore and we dried off in the sunshine, drinking beer.

'I could never leave Cornwall,' I said, taking a deep breath of the sea air.

Shane told me again about how he wanted to turn his life around. New job, new interests, less computer games. He said he was on the waiting list for a council house in St Ives which would make it easier for him to find work in a new town.

I leaned forward and gave him a lingering kiss of encouragement. If he believed he could change, I believed he could too. Everyone has the ability to change their ways, don't they?

Hope was the only thing I had left.

II

Honeymoon is Over

I thought I must still be dreaming as I woke up to see Shane's wardrobe on its side, barricading his bedroom door.

My heart went from sleepy to alert within seconds.

I'd had a few drinks with Lorraine the night before but everything was fine when I met up with Shane. He handed me his puffa jacket to keep warm and cuddled me the whole way home to his flat. I racked my brain to try and remember if we'd had an argument.

No, it was fine, everything was OK, and we were still in our happy phase together.

I could hear Shane was now awake from the change in his breathing but I was terrified to raise the alarm for fear of what was to come next. My heart was pounding as I played dumb by not showing I was trapped. It took all my courage to roll over, pretending I was still dozing.

I was now on my side, looking at the floor, staring at the six-inch carving knife that was lying next to me.

Oh God, oh God, why is there a knife on the floor?

My heart was now in my mouth and all I could hear was my breathing as the room closed in. I heard Shane stir behind me.

Oh God, oh God, I'm going to die.

He took a deep breath and turned to me. 'What's happened to your arm?' he asked, staring at my forearm.

What? I looked down and almost passed out.

'Oh my God,' I squealed. There were three cuts slashed down it. Each gash got deeper, longer, and had more blood seeping from it. I knew he had cut me, I knew it, but I couldn't say anything for fear of what he might do next. He'd trapped me in his room for a reason. He had a knife in there to hurt me.

'I don't know,' I said, playing dumb trying to mask my terror. I couldn't turn around and say, 'You've done this to me with your great big carving knife,' because he would smack me for speaking out.

'Huh,' he said. No expression on his face. His eyes were like a dead man's.

I lay there silent as a mouse, waiting for his next move. He kept staring at me and I kept playing along. I forced a smile to show him I wasn't scared. It felt insane to be pretending that waking up with a shredded arm and a wardrobe in front of the door was normal, but I had to. I was terrified of him.

Shane eventually peeled himself off his mattress and yanked the wardrobe back with his big tattooed arms. He strolled to the bathroom while I shook like a leaf under the covers.

Move, Tina! I pumped my body into action. I sprang out of bed and chucked on my smoky clothes from the night before.

'Going somewhere?' Shane asked as he caught me trying to make a getaway.

'No,' I lied, dropping my handbag to the floor. 'Just going to clean up my arm.'

I slunk off to his bathroom and winced with pain as I cleaned my gashes under the cold water. They weren't deep enough for stitching but the last cut was nasty. How could I have not felt him do it? Lorraine always used to say I was the deepest sleeper she had ever known, and I'd had a few drinks beforehand, so it seems like I'd slept through it.

I felt sick with the thought of his premeditated work – how he must have carefully sliced my arm and placed the knife by my side to taunt me. Why? We were doing so well, why did he have to ruin it again? I felt scared and confused, and firmly in Shane's grip.

'I could murder a fry-up,' Shane said as I came back into the room. It was like nothing had happened, and the best choice I could make was to go along with it. If he couldn't give me answers for the night he beat me up, there was no way I was going to get one out of him now. There was no way I was going to be stupid enough to provoke him.

'Let's go to the café,' I suggested, trying to sound extra-enthusiastic. I couldn't get out of there quick enough – my life had turned into something straight out of a horror film.

When I wasn't living horror, I was forced to see it on the television as Shane was watching more blood and gore than ever before. When he stayed around mine he would unfold my sofa bed in the living room and set up camp for the day and the night. I could have done all the chores, put the kids to bed, cooked and washed up before Shane looked up from the screen.

'Hey, check this out,' he said, zooming in on what looked like a milk carton.

'What is that?' I couldn't figure out what his latest fixation was. 'Looks like a carton to me,' I added, carrying on through to the kitchen.

'No, look,' he said excitedly as he enlarged the still from one of his zombie horrors. 'Pictures of all the missing people who've been savaged by zombies,' he said, his face lighting up.

'Oh, for God's sake,' I muttered.

I was saved by the bell as my doorbell went just in time. Shane pressed play and all I could hear from the living room was the shrill screams of innocent people being torn alive and Shane's bellowing laughter.

'Lorraine?' I wasn't expecting to see her on my doorstep. I quickly pulled my arm behind my back to hide the marks. I'd seen her briefly the other night but I'd been keeping my distance from my family over the past months.

'Hey, Tine, how are you?' Lorraine asked with a smile.

It was so nice to see her dimpled cheeks as I'd missed having her around. She clearly felt the same by turning up at my door, just like the old days.

'Cup of tea?' I enticed her in.

'Girl after my own heart,' she joked, stepping through.

'What?' I asked, as Lorraine stopped in her tracks. I knew exactly what – she had caught sight of Shane's trainers peeping out from the end of the sofa bed at the same time as I did.

'What is *he* doing here?' she fired at me.

Lorraine knew Shane was back in my life but had no idea to what extent. Her reaction was exactly why I'd kept myself to myself since May. I looked at her with my guilty blue eyes. I had no words to say to her.

'He's going to kill you,' she said, and then turned on her heels back down my drive.

Her words were like a javelin through my heart.

I wanted to call her back but I had nothing to say to her that would make her want to turn around. I wanted my sisters back, I missed them so much, but I needed Shane more. My body was literally craving for the times when he decided to be nice. I knew I was pathetic but I couldn't pull myself out of it.

More than anything, I dreaded losing Shane again to one of his booze benders where I didn't hear from him for days. The memory of lying awake praying he would call, imagining him getting off with all those girls, was more painful than remembering the bruises. It's so weird what makes your body crumble. I thought I knew myself but now I felt out of control.

I lingered at the door for a while longer until Lorraine disappeared from view. I could hear screams coming from the TV and I dreaded walking back in there.

'Ha, ha, brilliant,' Shane shouted, clapping his hands with delight.

I felt sick at the thought of what he was watching. Why do directors make these films? Surely they have to be warped themselves to come up with that sick stuff? I missed my romcoms and the Disney animations I used to watch with the kids before he took over.

I drew in a deep breath and braced myself.

'Look, look, T, check this out.' Shane was on the edge of his seat.

He was watching an old zombie classic which I swear he must have seen at least fifty times by now. He put it on slow motion so I knew I was in for a treat.

'Oh, oh, here it comes.'

My stomach turned as my 42-inch TV screen was filled with some guy's intestines being pulled apart.

'Wow, look at the graphics on that, it looks so amazing,' he said as he zoomed in on the gore.

I turned away, clutching my mouth.

'I'm going out in the garden,' I told him, using my hand as a blinker from the horror.

Shane was still revelling in it.

I stepped out into the sunshine but it wasn't warming me up like it usually did. I looked up to the sky and spotted the fading trails of passing planes but even the little things I used to take pleasure in were losing their sparkle.

I strolled to my trampoline and hoisted myself onto the springy platform. I unrolled my tense body and took a moment to try and relax. My body ached from stress but my mind wouldn't let it relax. I closed my eyes to absorb the sunshine but the images of the night before broke through.

I winced as I remembered Shane holding a hooked chef's knife to his face.

Go away. I tried to push the memory away but it was pointless to fight it.

I didn't remember what we had been arguing about, only that I was sitting up in bed when he stormed off downstairs. I waited nervously for my punishment as I could tell from the tone of his voice the fight wasn't going to end there.

I craned my ear to hear Shane opening and closing something in the kitchen. *Oh God, what now?* His behaviour had become so unpredictable I couldn't tell what he was going to do.

He could come back upstairs and kiss me, or kick me – it was like playing roulette, only the stakes were much higher.

He appeared at my panic room door, clutching something behind his back. His eyes were wild and glued on me. I played dumb by pretending to read my book, hoping that would calm the situation. He lingered there, forcing me to look up again, and as soon as he caught my eye, he pulled out his surprise.

My heart lurched. In his hand was one of my special chef's knives – the hooked one used for gutting fish intestines.

I played dumb. *Pretend you haven't seen it, pretend you're not scared shitless.*

He raised his arm to strike.

But not me this time – himself. He pulled the clawed knife down the side of his face, the whole time his eyes locked on me.

'No!' I screamed, leaping across the room. I grabbed the knife from his hand and threw it out of my bedroom window.

'What are you doing?' I demanded. I shook my head in disbelief.

Shane stood there like he had when I met him on the platform those many months ago – like a robot who didn't know what to do with his awkward big body. Blood was trickling down his sliced face onto my cream carpet.

'What have you done to yourself, Shane?' I said, tears welling in my eyes. I reached for his face but he backed off. 'Why are you hurting yourself?'

He stared at me blankly.

'Why?'

No answer.

But this time I understood what he was doing – he was trying to get my attention, just like my kids would have; only he was thirty years old not three years old. I grabbed some tissue from the bathroom and handed it to him. He seemed proud of his injury and reluctant to wipe away the damage.

'What am I going to do with you?' I mothered.

That was yesterday and today he was back watching the same old rubbish that I swear was warping his mind. I looked through the living room window at Shane, who was transfixed. He was broken goods and I didn't know whether I could fix him.

'Do you want a drink?' I asked from the kitchen as I came indoors to cool off.

'T, what do you think about this?' he beckoned.

What now? I thought, as I peered around the door. He turned away from the screen, revealing the slice down his face. Well, it was actually more like a scratch now. It's funny how he's more careful when it comes to harming himself, I thought.

'If the world had been taken over by zombies and we were the only survivors, what would you do if they were coming for us?'

'Huh?' What was he going on about?

'You know, zombies at your front door, climbing into your garden, smashing through the windows to tear us apart. What would you do?'

'Ummmm . . .' I was speechless.

'Well, I'd run up into the panic room and take out the stairs,' he said.

'What are you on about?' I shook my head.

'I'd be like bam bam bam,' he bragged, punching his clenched fists into the air.

'I don't think we'd stand a chance.' I tried to walk away from the ludicrous conversation.

'No, you're wrong,' Shane started to argue. He then talked about all the weapons he would use, the fight manoeuvres, how he would kill the living dead.

He spoke just like the motto on his Facebook page – 'You're coming with me, dead or alive'.

I'd get more sense from the worms in the garden, I thought as I left him midway through his rambling.

I could feel the prickles of tears burning in the back of my eyes. It made me so sad seeing him like that and so helpless to repair him. The trouble with me is that all my life I've been determined to do the impossible. If someone told me I couldn't make a jump when I was horse riding I'd try and jump the stile three times over. I'd seen what Shane could be and believed if I tried hard enough I could make 'us' work.

As Shane's cut healed so did our relationship as we fell into another couple of honeymoon weeks. I cooked him meals, he was caring and loving, and he made an extra effort with Ben and Liam. I did my best to blank out the bad and I focused on the good.

The news that there was a massive manhunt for a guy who had shot his ex-girlfriend, her boyfriend and blinded a cop with a sawn-off shotgun was all over the TV and papers. Shane was never interested in watching the news but he was transfixed by this story. Raoul Moat was quickly becoming his hero for declaring war on the police.

'Yes, yes!' Shane clapped his hands as he watched the report about how Moat fired his shotgun in PC David Rathband's face just because he was a cop.

'That is awful,' I gasped, shrinking into the sofa in horror.

'No, that's good. He's police, so he deserved it.' Shane was the most excited I'd seen him in months.

Just because he'd done time and been in trouble with the police, he thought they were his enemy. I hated him for this. Seeing his face light up at someone else's misery made me furious.

'That's not good, that cop has got kids, he's got a wife,' I argued.

Shane ignored me.

'He was doing a job at the end of the day. If there wasn't police there would be anarchy,' I went on.

Shane wasn't interested. Moaty was his hero.

I couldn't get much sense out of Shane for those six days Moat was on the run. I woke up at 1.00 a.m. to an empty bed on our Friday night together – Shane was still downstairs watching TV.

'This is bloody ridiculous,' I muttered, pulling the sheets off and throwing on my dressing gown. I tiptoed into the living room to see him glued to a live report. He was so mesmerised he didn't even notice I'd come in.

'Hello, you are watching Sky News with live coverage of the stand-off between the fugitive Raoul Moat and armed police officers,' the reporter announced.

'The man called Britain's Most Wanted is surrounded by at least ten snipers in the riverside area of Rothbury in Northumberland. Witnesses say he is holding a sawn-off shot-gun to his head and sometimes to his throat,' she read out from what looked like a car park full of riot vans and police cars.

'Go on, get 'em,' Shane shouted at the TV like it was a football match.

My living room was soon filled with the sound of gunfire and someone shouting.

'Come on!' Shane was on the edge of his seat, clapping.

'What we heard less than a minute ago was gunshots and frantic shouting,' a police officer reported.

'That's right, you take 'em out, son.' Shane was almost drooling. I didn't know what was more disturbing – the breaking news or watching Shane.

'We can confirm that gunshots have been fired and the suspect has a gunshot wound,' the officer read out.

'No,' Shane sighed, running his hands over his shaved head.

'About bloody time,' I chirped up as a convoy of ambulances appeared on the screen.

Shane turned around to face me. His eyes were wild with excitement.

'I'm going to do a Raoul Moat,' he said. 'I'm going to get a gun and shoot up the police station.'

'You are joking?' I couldn't believe what he was saying. My boyfriend was nuts.

'I'm serious, T,' he insisted. 'I'm going to be taken down in a blaze of glory.'

12

Panic Room

'Come on, Ben, it's way past your bedtime,' I told my eldest, trying to get him upstairs.

'Muuuuuum,' he whined. He was enjoying playing computer games with Shane.

'No, Ben, now.' I crossed my arms and waited by the door.

'Give the poor guy a break, we're nearly finished,' Shane interfered.

It was the straw that broke the camel's back for me, as when it came to my kids what I said went. The tension over the weeks had been building but I never allowed it to vent for fear of the hiding I'd get for opening my mouth. Every volcano erupts in the end though.

'I don't think you're in a position to tell me how to raise my kids,' I snapped. As soon as I said it I wanted to take the words back. Shane's eyes flared up.

I sidled off to the kitchen to cool off as the temperature in the living room had suddenly rocketed.

'Come on, Ben,' I yelled again, staring out the kitchen window into the starry night sky.

I felt his presence even before I saw his reflection in the window. A chill trickled down my spine; I knew what was coming. Shane swooped up behind me and pushed me into the cupboard, sending me buckling over the sink.

A shot of adrenalin injected into my heart and I sprinted for the back door.

'HELP! HELP!' I screamed into the blackness.

Two stomps and he was on my back again. He grabbed me by the scruff of my jumper, lifted me up and flung me backwards. I crashed onto the kitchen floor, hitting my head. BANG!

I couldn't see. I held my hands in front of my face and felt them trembling. The room went quiet and all I could hear was my heartbeat . . . and then his footsteps – THUD, THUD – and then his big hand came down.

'No, please,' I begged.

Shane grabbed me and dragged me back into the living room.

'Muuuum,' Ben screamed as he cowered on the sofa.

I couldn't speak to tell him Mummy was going to be OK.

Shane threw me down on the other sofa and slam-dunked his body on me like a WWF wrestler. My lungs felt like they had exploded under his huge body.

'Get off my mum!' Ben screamed. I couldn't see him but I could imagine his terrified face.

Still without saying a word, Shane wrapped his legs around mine so I was trapped. I felt like I was in a vice about to be snapped in two and the tension tore through my body.

'Get off my mum, let her go!' Ben was screaming so loud his voice had turned into a rasp. I craned my neck to look at him as my vision slowly returned. My poor Ben was shivering, tears were streaming. I needed to get this monster off me and help my boy.

'Shut up,' Shane said. His eyes were black. 'If you move, I'll break your legs,' he told me. He was so matter of fact about his torture.

I was trying to stifle my cries so Ben couldn't see my pain.

'Please, Shane,' I begged. 'Please.'

The light in the room was fading. I was about to pass out.

BANG! BANG! BANG!

Someone pounded at my front door. Shane jumped off me and stood in the middle of the living room, not knowing what to do next.

BANG! BANG! BANG!

'It's the police,' a gruff voice shouted. My neighbours must have reported Ben crying. Shane bolted up my stairs and locked himself inside my panic room.

'It's going to be OK, Ben,' I reassured my baby with a hug before staggering to the door. My body felt like a lead weight.

'Mr Jenkin here?' asked the policeman. Behind him a dozen cops were lined up outside, ready to raid my house.

Shane was breaking his bail conditions by being at my house. Minutes ago he was about to break my legs. If I didn't lie for him he'd hurt me again. I was shaking with fear.

'No, he ain't,' I said.

'We're coming in anyway,' the officer insisted, stepping forward.

Like a cornered animal, I fought back: 'You need a warrant to search my premises.'

'No we don't, love.' The cop flung open my door, and they charged in like a herd of elephants; some ran into the living room, the others stomped upstairs.

BANG! BANG! BANG!

'Open the door, Mr Jenkin, we know you're in there,' they demanded, pounding on my bedroom door.

I chased up after them but my heart stopped as I saw a trail of blood going up the stairs.

Has he hurt himself? Has he cut himself?

'SHANE!' I screamed.

Ben was now by my side, crying.

'Shane, are you OK?' I yelled again.

A policewoman led us into the kids' bedroom and told me to wait on Ben's bed. She guarded the exit like a Rottweiler. Ben huddled into me and I wrapped my arms tightly around his quivering body. I kissed his forehead and felt sick with guilt. I had caused all this, this was all my fault.

But the memory of Shane slicing his face with my knife took over. I imagined him on my bed cutting himself to shreds.

'Are you all right, Shane?' I shouted. I rose to my feet but the cop pushed me back on the bed.

No answer. My thoughts went into overdrive.

'Just open the door,' I pleaded. I got up again but the WPC pushed me down.

Ben was crying and Liam was screaming in his cot.

'Come on, lads, on the count of three,' I heard a cop say. The officers attacked my door with a battering ram.

BOSH! And then BOSH! And then BOSH!

'Whaaaaaah!' Liam wailed.

BOSH! BOSH! BOSH!

But still not a peep out of Shane. What if he'd killed himself?

BOSH! Whaaaaaah! My head was going to explode with the noise.

'We're in,' the police celebrated as they took my door off its hinges.

'Stay where you are,' they ordered Shane. 'Lie down on your front with your hands behind your back.'

I could hear the sound of handcuffs locking and then Shane appeared. His dream of going out in a blaze of glory like Moaty was getting closer.

He looked at me and then away like I was nothing. That gut-wrenching feeling that it was all my fault returned.

'Are you all right?' I asked as I chased after them down the stairs.

He wouldn't answer me.

'Shane, are you OK?'

By ignoring me he made me even more afraid of him. I needed him to forgive me, to know he still loved me.

'Are we still together?' I whimpered. My last ounce of dignity, gone.

That got his attention. 'Yeah, we're still together,' he said.

Tears of relief filled my eyes as I watched him taken off by the police.

13

Breakdown

I'd been paralysed for two days waiting for news from Shane. Finally my mobile went off. It was an unknown number. It had to be him, please be him.

'Hi, T.' His familiar voice was like a soothing ointment on burns.

'Where are you?'

'I'm in the nick, Exeter Prison. Don't know how long I'm gonna be in here for,' he said.

'But you're OK?' I needed to know he wasn't hurt.

'Yeah, cut my foot on your stairs, that was all.'

'I was so worried about you,' I quivered.

He paused for a minute and I could hear his breath on the other end of the line.

'I hope you'll wait for me,' he said softly. I was talking to the Shane I loved. 'I want us to be together, as soon as this is all sorted we won't have to hide any more.'

My stomach somersaulted with happiness at the thought of a perfect life together.

'I'll sort my life out.'

Promises.

'I'll get a job and I'll take care of you.'

More promises.

'I told you I'd wait,' I reassured him. 'I'll stand by you, but as soon as all this stuff is over and done with, no more of this.

'NO MORE,' I crumbled.

Even a phone conversation with Shane exhausted me. I was running on empty as I was barely eating because I was too busy worrying about Shane and too busy trying to take care of my boys.

I was expecting social services to come knocking – it was just a matter of time.

I was on my own at home when the dreaded day came. A short plump lady with shoulder-length mousy hair stood on my doorstep explaining she was a social worker from the council who had been alerted to a 'situation'.

'Can I come in please, Miss Nash?' she asked. I didn't have a choice. I knew she was only doing her job but I didn't warm to her and I was petrified she was going to take my kids away from me. She said she was concerned for the safety of my children since Shane broke his bail conditions and was caught in my house.

I sat on the edge of the seat, my hands nervously clasped between my knees.

I wanted to shout at her and tell her Shane would never hurt my kids. It was me he got angry with and that was often my fault.

'Miss Nash, you reported a very serious attack on yourself,' she started.

'I never,' I butted in.

I recited the story Shane had drilled into me.

'Shane didn't hit me that night, I got jealous and had a go at him. I tripped and fell down the stairs.'

I was almost believing it now.

'He's not dangerous,' I insisted.

The social worker glared at me like a stern schoolteacher. She drew in a deep breath and took a long look around the room as if she was inspecting for clues to my madness.

'He's a dangerous man . . .' Her words hung in the air.

My palms were now glued together with my nervous sweat.

'Well, tell me his history then?' I argued.

'We can't disclose that for legal reasons,' she said, like she'd rehearsed it.

He won't hurt my kids, he just hurts me, don't take my kids from me, please don't take my kids.

After an hour of bartering the social worker slurped her last drop of cold tea and got up to leave.

'We'll have to have another review; with you and Shane together,' she said, looking at me as if to say this wasn't the last I'd see of her.

'Yep, fine, I'll do anything you want.' I couldn't get her out of my house fast enough.

As soon as she left I burst into tears. My whole body was shaking like I was trapped in the cold. I shuffled through to my living room and collapsed on the sofa. I hadn't prayed to God since Mum forced us to go to Sunday school and read the Bible in bed. I was that scared, I needed him now.

'Please, God, don't let them take my kids.' I bowed my head above my clasped hands. My tears splashed into my lap.

I'd tried my best to keep my distance, but I needed my family more than ever. I threw on my jacket and ran down to Nan's. She took one look at my red puffy eyes and cradled me into her cosy living room.

'They're going to take my kids off me,' I sobbed. 'Social services want to take them away because of Shane.'

Nan reached out her creased arm and squeezed my hands firmly. She still had quite a grip on her even after all these years.

'Over our dead bodies,' she said. There was no messing with my nan when she got mad. 'Those kids aren't going anywhere, you're a good mum.'

'Thanks, Nan,' I sniffled.

'Now dry those tears,' she told me.

'Yes, Nan,' I replied, wiping my eyes.

She poured me a cup of tea and straightened the creases on her tablecloth. She sighed deeply and told me what was on her mind.

'You need to get rid of that awful boyfriend of yours, though. He's a wrong 'un.'

'I know, Nan,' I said, doubting I'd ever have the strength to do it.

'You can't be letting him back in your house or social services will take your kids,' she warned.

'I know, I know.' I realised I shouldn't let Shane set foot in my house ever again.

'OK, now have some cake, dear, you look starving.' Nan pushed a slice my way.

'Thanks, Nan.'

I was lucky I had such an amazing family who loved me despite everything I had put them through. I hated myself but

I didn't know how to escape the mess I'd made. Shane was like an anchor, stopping me from sailing away. I couldn't tell Nan that I was desperate for Shane to come out of prison and be back in my arms. He sounded so sincere this time about changing his life, wanting a new future for us. I vowed to stop provoking him. I reflected on how I would wind him up. Surely it was my fault that he was always getting angry and striking out.

I was in limbo while Shane was in prison. I stayed at home looking after the boys, daydreaming about what Shane might be doing, if he was OK, when he would be coming out. It had been a week since he called and I wanted to let him know he couldn't come anywhere near my house again.

'Bang-bang.' I was woken from my thoughts by the front door.

It was Shane. What the hell?

'Get in here,' I said, pulling him inside. I peered out the window to check no one was watching. My whole body was trembling.

'Oh my God, what are you doing here?' I was shaking. I was so happy to see him but mad that he was risking everything.

'I wanted to surprise you. I got the train from Exeter this morning,' he said, pulling me close.

'Shane, no, please, they'll take my kids if they know you're here.' I was trying to fight his embrace.

'They won't take your kids away, they can't, you aren't a bad mum, you haven't neglected them.' I could feel the testosterone bubbling as he thought about how much he hated the system.

'Shane, please, they mean everything to me,' I begged, even as I melted into him.

'I've missed you so much,' he said, and kissed me. 'I love you.' He kissed me again. 'I haven't stopped talking about you, all my mates in there know how much I love you.'

'Really?' I giggled. He could make me feel so special when he tried. He just had to switch on his charm and I was putty in his hands. I just wanted to be loved by him.

He squeezed me into his broad chest so I could barely breathe and kissed my forehead. He told me again how when this was all over we were going to start a new life together. He made it seem like it was us versus the rest of the world, just like something out of his zombie films.

'We'll be together soon,' I reassured him.

'We just need to get the cops off my back,' he sighed, making me feel guilty again.

'I'll do whatever you want.'

He grinned and pulled me by my hand up to the bedroom. I lost count of how many times we made love that day and night. There were so many emotions flying around that the sex was incredible. I didn't know how long we'd have together before the next drama exploded, so every second felt precious. I woke up early the next morning, worried sick the police would catch Shane in my house. I left him sleeping while I crept downstairs to have a glass of water. I needed a cigarette to calm my nerves but my fingers were shaking so badly I couldn't light the bloody thing.

'Come on,' I said, flicking the lighter.

BANG! BANG! BANG!

I froze with fear.

BANG! BANG! BANG! Again on my front door. I'd turned into a statue – glass of water in one hand, cigarette in the other.

BANG! BANG! On my front room window this time.

I moved my head to see a copper staring at me.

'Can you open the door please, love,' he said.

'Oh yeah, OK.' I shook myself out of my trance.

I pulled open my front door to see a small army of police officers lined up.

'Can we come in?' It wasn't really a question.

'Do I have a choice?' I said, crossing my arms defensively.

'No,' the officer in charge said, barging past me. They streamed into my house again – it was like déjà vu. I followed them upstairs and watched as they closed in on Shane. He seemed to be taking it in his stride as he made them wait while he slowly put on his rugby top and jogging bottoms. He looked up at me and I shook my head as if to say, 'I can't believe this is happening again'. They cuffed him and led him out and I was left to pick up the pieces, again.

Shane was sent back to prison for breaching bail conditions, only to turn up on my doorstep again a few days later. He wasn't listening to a word I was saying. Why wasn't it sinking in that he had to stay away from my house? He didn't seem to care whether I lost my kids.

'Close all the curtains,' Shane ordered. 'That way no one can see I'm here.'

His eyes were wild with excitement. I could tell he was getting a thrill from breaking the law. It was like he wanted the police to hunt him down. He wanted to go out in a 'blaze of glory' like Raoul Moat. He followed me into every room, watching me draw the curtains.

'Is that OK?' I asked. He was scaring me.

He nodded and signalled me to go upstairs and take care of the rest of the house. I switched on the hall light to see what I was doing and he went wild.

'No lights!' he shouted. No one was allowed to know that we were in.

'But how are we going to see? The boys need to be able to see,' I pleaded.

'They can have a candle in their room,' Shane said, peering through a gap in the curtain to check if cops were watching.

Shane had left prison only to turn my house into a prison. I wasn't even allowed to go to the shops for food in case the cops followed me. I did what I was told though – there was no way I was going to argue with Shane while he was in one of these moods.

I lit a candle, scooped Liam into my arms and carried him up to his cot.

'Mum, why can't we have the lights on?' Ben asked innocently as I placed Liam down and kissed his head goodnight.

'It's just for tonight, nothing to worry about.' I tried to sound calm as I sat next to Ben on his bed.

'Is everything OK, Mum?' Ben's eyes were big and sad.

I felt like someone had pulled out my heart and stamped on it. My poor babies, what have I done? The tears welled in my eyes and I hugged Ben to stop him seeing his mummy cry.

'Everything is great,' I lied, squeezing him like I never wanted to let go.

'I'll check on you later,' I said as I rose to my feet. I wobbled my way back downstairs, feeling faint from lack of food and nervous exhaustion. I'd tucked my kids in and now I had to attend to the big kid downstairs.

The living room was pitch-black except for the flickering TV. So I wasn't allowed the lights on but he was allowed to light up the room with his bloody horror films. I didn't have the energy to fight it. I collapsed on the sofa and curled into Shane's chest. My eyelids were too heavy to keep open, they rolled down like shutters, and I fell asleep to the soft murmur of Shane's heartbeat.

BANG! BANG! BANG! The cops were back at my door.

'Open up,' they shouted.

'I can't take this any more, Shane,' I trembled. 'You've got to stay away.'

Shane puffed out his chest as the cops came for him. He smirked as they cuffed his hands behind his back.

'This isn't funny, Shane,' I told him, shaking my head with despair.

Shane was carted back to prison and I was left a nervous wreck to pick up the pieces.

Social services were back on my case a day later and I had to explain to them again how the restraining order Shane was breaking was all my fault in the first place – I'd beaten him up out of jealousy. I know they didn't believe me, that's why they kept coming back to trip me up.

'I'm a good mother,' I pleaded with the lady. 'Ask anyone, they will tell you I'm a good mother.' I was so exhausted I was tripping up on my words.

'I'll be back, Miss Nash,' the woman from social services threatened.

I closed the door on her but I couldn't relax. I'd turned into a bundle of nerves, jumping at every sound, thinking it was the police bashing down my door, Shane turning up or social services knocking. I sat on the edge of my seat, paralysed, with hands clasped between my knees, waiting for something to happen.

I couldn't eat, I couldn't sleep, I wasn't taking care of the way I looked – my blonde hair was greasy and scraped back into a ponytail. My cheeks were hollow, the bags below my eyes were purple from tiredness – I looked a wreck. I was using my last ounce of energy to look after my boys.

My mobile went off – it was an unknown number, it had to be him.

'T, I'm going to be at yours in a minute,' Shane warned me.

'No, Shane, you can't,' I started, but he'd already hung up.

14

Christmas from Hell

'When are we going to start trying for a baby?' Shane rolled on top of me.

I giggled nervously.

'Have you been to the doctor to see about having your coil removed?' he badgered.

'Yeah, I will,' I said, trying to fob him off.

'Well, hurry up and sort it.' His voice flickered with anger.

'I will.' I played dumb again. He must be joking if he thought I was going to add being pregnant to the 101 worries I already had.

But when Shane got an idea in his head he became obsessed and I wouldn't hear the end of it for weeks. We were at his place because the police had finally put him on tag on 5 November, which meant an alarm was triggered if he set foot near my house in Hayle. It meant I got to see him less often, only when Paul had the kids twice a week. Shane was making up for lost time as he pulled at my clothes.

'I love you, let's make a baby,' he insisted as he touched me.

I smothered his mouth with my kisses to stop him talking. He gently stroked between my legs and then he slipped his fingers inside me. I arched my back in ecstasy. He pushed his fingers deep, deeper, taking my breath away. He thrust harder and started to burrow with his nails.

I shot up from the bed in agony.

'Oh no, you're not doing that,' I gasped, realising what he was trying to do – pull my coil out.

I'd had a coil removed before by a doctor once before and it left me feeling like I had been punched in the stomach. I couldn't believe he was trying to do the same with his bare hands.

'Ha, ha,' he laughed, and looked as if to say 'I'll get you next time'.

I crossed my arms and he tugged at my leg in his childish way.

'Come on, T,' he said, trying to win me over.

I glared at him with mistrusting eyes. I was on edge all the time from never knowing what Shane was going to do next. I was exhausted from trying my hardest not to upset him, from trying to anticipate the things that might anger him and from trying to fix them before he beat the crap out of me. He grabbed my ankle and with one tug he pulled me down the bed. It was pointless to resist. I let him touch me and take me.

We'd been having a good week in the run-up to Christmas. We hadn't fought and he hadn't broken his bail for over a month. Shane had rekindled his relationship with his mum since his dad still refused to speak to him. I was going to spend Christmas Day with both of them at her flat in Penzance after I'd had the morning with my boys. I couldn't wait to see Shane's face when he unwrapped my presents, which I'd spent months saving up for. I'd spent hundreds of pounds on them, the most I'd done for any boyfriend.

I laughed to myself as I remembered last Christmas when Shane had decorated his flat from top to toe in tinsel and balloons, and I hoped to make this year as special as that. I had this overriding need to please him all the time that I couldn't explain.

I woke up at the crack of dawn so I could start preparing an early dinner for the boys. I wanted to make the day extra-special to make up for all the drama over the past months.

'Mum, can I open my presents now?' Ben asked, creeping up on me.

'No, Ben, you have to wait.' I tickled him as he reached under the Christmas tree.

'Pleeeeease,' he begged, feeling his presents.

'OK, you can open one and then the rest after dinner.'

Ben dived for the biggest present and ripped off the wrapping paper. I switched on my Christmas album and then danced my way up the stairs to pick Liam out of his cot.

'Where's Shane?' Liam asked as I scooped him up in my arms. He was missing Shane not being around all the time.

'Shane wishes you Merry Christmas,' I said, and kissed Liam's button nose.

The boys were picked up just before noon by Paul, and a friend of mine, who lived on the estate, offered to drive me into Penzance because I hadn't been able to fix my Peugeot after Shane smashed it up. I had straightened my hair, done my make-up and splashed my favourite perfume on just for Shane.

'You smell nice,' said Wendy as I climbed into the car with my bag full of presents.

'That Shane is a very lucky guy, you're a saint to put up with him.' She didn't know the half of it. No one did, as I'd kept my life a secret for months. I'd barely been allowed out of my house for the weeks Shane was in and out of prison.

Shane didn't have a mobile so he'd given me his mum's number to call when I was heading down. 'I'm almost there,' I texted excitedly. I put my mobile back in my handbag, not expecting a reply.

'Beep beep,' my phone bleeped.

My heart sank.

'Shane isn't here, he hasn't been here all night,' his mum texted back.

'I don't believe it,' I stammered.

'What's wrong?' Wendy asked. She slowed down, assuming I'd forgotten to pack a present.

'He's not there, he's not bloody there.' I couldn't stop the tears, I'd been looking forward to this moment for weeks. I thought it would be the one day of our relationship which he wouldn't dare to spoil.

'He doesn't give a shit. Take me back to Hayle.'

I walked into the empty echo of my front hall and dropped my bag of presents on the floor. I couldn't believe it – I was spending Christmas Day by myself. I crawled onto the sofa and cuddled under Liam's quilt while I waited for Shane to get in touch.

One hour passed. Two hours. Three hours, and still no news. I couldn't even call my sisters because they were all busy opening presents with their boyfriends. I would have been too embarrassed to tell them Shane had let me down, again.

More hours went by and I was now sitting in the dark with just the flickering TV for company. My phone finally rang. I knew it would be him and I knew I shouldn't answer.

'Hello?' I picked up.

'Merry Christmas.'

'Fuck you, Shane.' I was livid.

'What? I had a big night out last night,' was his excuse. No sorry, no real explanation.

'You bastard. You ruined my Christmas,' I screamed down the phone. I didn't care if he beat me for saying my piece; I'd been looking forward to this day for months. Shane wasn't used to me getting mad, and for the first time I heard fear in his voice.

'I'll come over,' he said.

'Stay away from me,' I rasped, and slammed down the phone.

I thought I meant it, but as more hours passed, I just wished I was in Shane's arms watching tacky Christmas TV together. It was 9 p.m. when he finally turned up on my doorstep.

'Go away,' I shouted, barring him from coming in. 'You're on tag, you're not allowed here.'

'Don't be pissed off, T,' he said, teasing me with his bag of presents. 'It's not my fault, I stayed around a mate's last night.' He showed me his puppy-dog whimper face.

'You ruined my Christmas,' I repeated, but I was already starting to back down. Every time he kept me waiting and guessing, I was left a nervous wreck desperate for his reassurance that we were going to be OK, that we were still together.

I stepped back and let him into my house. I didn't know how long we would have together before the police came knocking, so we had to make the most of it. I switched the Christmas tree lights back on and handed over his bag full of presents.

My heart lit up as I watched him open up present after present. I'd bought him Paco Rabanne aftershave, a jacket, a yellow

Nike T-shirt, a cuddly toy – hours of thought had gone into choosing them. He leaned forward and planted a strong kiss on my lips.

'I love this,' he said, squirting his aftershave over his neck.

'I've got something else for you too,' he said, pulling out a surprise present from behind his back.

'What is it?' I jiggled the small box. Then I carefully unwrapped the bow and lifted the lid.

'Oh, Shane, it's beautiful,' I gushed, holding up the gold heart necklace. Shane had told me he'd never bought jewellery for a girl before, so he must love me. This was the sign I needed. I lunged forward and wrapped my tiny arms around his thick neck.

'I love you,' I whispered, kissing him gently. He smiled shyly, revealing the vulnerable Shane I adored.

I woke the next morning with that familiar gnawing sensation in my stomach, the nausea I got when I felt something was wrong. I couldn't forget how Shane had ruined our Christmas together – no gold necklace could fix it.

'What's up with you?' Shane asked, irritated I wasn't in the mood for sex.

'Nothing,' I said, getting out of bed. I'd learned how to keep my mouth shut but sometimes I still found it hard to fake a smile.

'Moody bitch,' he snapped.

'What?'

'You heard,' he provoked.

There was going to be a fight whether I liked it or not. I reminded him how badly he had let me down and he turned. His lip snarled up like a dog and his eyes turned black. I edged away from him and instead of reaching for me, he grabbed his presents. He held up his Nike Air T-shirt and started shredding it in front of me. He tore the arms and legs off his teddy bear, the filling flying everywhere.

'No,' I cried out as he went for the jacket. He laughed as he ripped it apart. I couldn't watch, I'd spent a small fortune on it. He then waited for me to look up so he could catch my eye. He smirked as he lifted his aftershave above his head and then tipped it all over himself.

'You bastard.' I couldn't take any more.

'GET OUT OF MY HOUSE!' I screamed so loud the street must have heard.

He rolled his head back as he cackled with laughter.

'Get the fuck out of my house!' I never usually swore but watching him demolish the things I'd saved so hard to buy him hurt more than his fists.

He walked backwards to my door, taunting me by jiggling the bottle.

'Get out of my house, Shane,' I sobbed, tears streaming down my face.

He tipped the remainder of the aftershave over his head as I pushed him onto the porch. I cried my eyes out after he left. I'd had the worst Christmas of my life. I took off his necklace and threw it across the room in rage. 'Fuck you, Shane Jenkin,' I wept.

I spent the next few days fending off the police, who came knocking on my door looking for Shane because his tag had given him away.

'I have no idea where he is,' I told them, which was the truth this time.

As the days went by without Shane, time seemed to slow right down. Every minute was filled with thoughts of him. I'd try and busy myself cleaning the house, going to the shops, seeing Nan, but after a while even that stopped working. I'd find myself staring into space dreaming up jealous thoughts of who Shane might be with. He knew exactly how to play me – that if he stayed away for long enough I'd come begging for his love. But it's one thing knowing how someone controls you, and another knowing how to actually break free from it.

Shane finally turned up on my doorstep late evening on 29 December when I was already in bed. He smelled like he hadn't washed for days, he had four days' stubble and his eyes were wild with that hunted look he got when the police were after him. He was twitchy and argumentative and I had a sinking feeling there would be trouble later. Luckily the boys were with Paul for the night.

'Come up,' I said, leading him to my room. I needed to lie down; I was exhausted from all the worrying I'd been doing over the past four days. I crawled back into bed and propped up the pillows behind me to help me stay awake.

'So are you going to say sorry?' I finally asked.

'What for?' he shrugged.

'For ripping up my presents.'

Shut up, Tina, I screamed in my head. My words were like waving a red rag in front of a bull, and more than anything I wanted to take them back.

'I'm sorry,' I begged, but it was too late. Shane bounded across the room like a tiger and jumped on me, trapping me underneath his giant body. He locked me between his thighs and then he closed in on my face with his hands, his thumbs poised like shovels about to scoop my eyes out.

I froze with fear. I opened my mouth to scream but no sound came out.

'Please,' I managed to whisper.

His hands stopped and hovered above my face, as if he was thinking about whether to do it or not. His shovels turned into claws as he scratched down my cheeks instead. His eyes were as black as the night. I grabbed the duvet and threw it over my head, hoping that would save me.

Shane wasn't interested in my eyes any more though, he wanted to hurt me in a different way this time. He backed off and headed to the corner of my room where I kept my beloved DJ decks. He made sure I was watching as he raised his fists into the air.

'Nooooo!' I screamed as the gorilla in front of me punched my turntables. Wood and metal went flying as he smashed them to smithereens.

My face was going to be next. I leaped out of bed and ran to my bedroom window facing the street.

'HELP!' I screamed.

The alarm scared him and Shane sprinted down the stairs. I chased him out the house and slammed the door as he ran up the street.

Why does he keep going for my eyes?

I covered my heart with my hand as if that would stop it trembling its way out of my body. Everything fell quiet – too quiet – it was like I was in a horror film waiting for the monster to jump out and get me.

BANG! BANG! BANG!

I nearly leaped out of my skin as Shane thumped his fists on my door.

'Open the door, Tina!' he yelled.

'Leave me alone,' I shouted, cowering on the other side.

But Shane wouldn't give up, he kept shouting and banging and kicking, calling me every name under the sun. I tried to be brave but I was shaking like a leaf. Then, suddenly, it all fell silent again. I waited on tenterhooks by the front door for it all to kick off.

The fighter in me finally snapped. I'm not letting him turn me into a prisoner in my own home, I thought. I stomped upstairs to survey the damage. The decks were broken beyond repair. It had taken me years to save up for them and he'd smashed them in seconds. Shane knew how much they meant to me, which was exactly why he'd attacked them. First my presents and now my decks – bit by bit he was destroying me.

I rolled my shaking body out on the bed and lay there rigidly waiting for Round 3.

'Open the fucking door!' Shane bellowed, waking up the street. 'Let me in!'

BANG! BANG! BANG!

I peeled myself off the mattress and opened the window onto the cold winter night. It must have been getting on past 1 a.m.

'Leave me alone. I'm not afraid of you,' I lied.

'Let me in, bitch!' he shouted under my window.

I'm not letting you scare me, I'm not letting you scare me.

I lay back down on the bed, my body poised, ready to run at any moment. I tried to block out his shouting by imagining I was floating high above myself, looking down on the pathetic Tina I had become. Everything turned deathly silent again and all I could hear was my panicked breath. In, out, in, out. I closed my eyes to try and calm my galloping heart.

Baboom!

Out of nowhere a massive rock smashed through my window, raining shards of glass down on me. It flew across to the other side of the room, bounced off the adjacent window frame and came to rest next to me on my bed.

'What the . . . ?'

I couldn't believe it, he had torn my presents to pieces, smashed my decks and now smashed my bedroom window. I tried to lift my arms but with every move I felt needles of glass stabbing into me. You can do this, Tina, I told myself. I had to move, I had to get up. One, two, three, I counted myself down. I winced with agony, the shards impaling the soles of my feet as I edged around the mattress. I didn't know where I was going, I was just moving to stay alive. Relief flooded over me as I heard the sound of police sirens closing in. I managed to make it to the window in time to see Shane running off down the street.

The police questioned me for hours and this time I told them the truth about what happened; I didn't have the energy to lie any more.

'Do you know where he is, Miss Nash?' the police officer asked me.

I shook my head.

'Well, when we catch him, and we will catch him, Miss Nash, he'll be going straight back to prison.'

I nodded.

When the police finally left I spent the next hour pulling pieces of glass out of my feet. I staggered into Ben's bed and caught a few hours' sleep before sunrise. I didn't know what a nervous breakdown felt like but I was pretty sure I was having one.

I'd started to love sleeping more than living because it was the only time I could forget how my life was falling to pieces. I dreaded that gut-wrenching feeling in the morning when I had to relive everything that had happened the night before.

'Oh my God,' I whimpered when I opened my bedroom door. The room looked like a bomb site with glass everywhere. Two years ago I would have had a fit if a dirty cup was left out; I couldn't believe how far my standards had fallen. I slid down the wall into a heap and kicked one of Liam's toys down the stairs in anger.

'Fuck you, Shane Jenkin,' I whispered. I had no anger left, just sadness.

As the days passed I slipped into depression. I could barely pull myself out of bed to get the kids to school. I couldn't sleep and I couldn't stop crying. I felt guilty for what I had done and the only person who could mend my heart was the man who was breaking it.

I'm sorry, Shane, I'm sorry, Shane. I found myself practising the words in the quiet lonely moments of the day. It was my fault for bringing up the presents; I should have left it as he already had enough on his plate. I was looking gaunt and brittle when Shane eventually came knocking.

He looked even worse than the time before and he smelled like he'd been drinking away his problems. His eyes were sad and I could tell he was sorry. My maternal instinct kicked in and I just wanted to look after him.

'Come here,' I said, reaching my arms around his neck for a hug. I had to stand on my tiptoes he was so tall.

He shuffled forward like a lost boy as I brought him in from the cold.

'Can I stay the night?' he begged.

I breathed deeply as I built up the courage to say my bit. I'd reached breaking point and he knew it.

'You can stay, but tomorrow you have to hand yourself into the police.' I couldn't look him in the eye, otherwise I'd cry.

'You have to, Shane, I can't take any more of this. If the police catch you here I'll have my kids taken away from me.'

He nodded; he knew he'd gone too far.

I didn't know how long he would be going inside for this time as the police had warned me he had breached his bail so many times, and clocked up so many further offences, they might keep him in prison until his Crown Court hearing on 14 February. We couldn't let each other go all night. If I rolled over in bed his hands would find me and pull me back into his warm chest.

I woke up early and spent a while watching him sleep, taking in my last moments of his beautiful body. He looked so peaceful, a far cry from the monster who had been terrorising me a few days ago. He must have felt my gaze upon him as he rolled over and kissed me. I had to bite my cheek to stop myself from crying.

Shane left early and we spent our last minutes together hugging and kissing on my doorstep. We didn't want to let each other go. He lifted his hand up to my face – but this time to sweep my hair behind my ear.

'I'm going to hand myself in.' His mouth quivered as he spoke. 'And I'm going to sort myself out. I'm going to get a job, everything will change,' he promised.

My lip started to tremble.

'I love you,' he said. 'I'm fed up of arguing. If we love each other, why are we arguing?'

I shrugged. The truth was because he had a violent temper, but I didn't want to deal with the truth.

I hugged him and tears welled in my eyes.

'OK, I'm going to go and sort this out,' he said, finally breaking away.

'I love you.' I pulled him back into my arms – I wasn't ready to let him go.

'I hope you'll wait for me,' he mumbled, his eyes full of sadness.

Tears rolled down my cheeks, bleeding into the shoulder of his top. It was a freezing January morning but I couldn't feel the cold.

'You know I will, I just want you to sort yourself,' I told him.

He pulled back and I watched him walk away.

'I love you, Shane Jenkin,' I whispered.

15

Break Away

Although I missed Shane, I was also glad he'd handed himself in because I needed a break. I'd been running on empty for months and my body showed it. My hair was greasy and had inch-long dark roots. My skin was grey and lifeless. I had shopping bags under my eyes from sleep deprivation. I weighed less than eight stone and my hip bones were now jutting through. I looked forty years old, not thirty.

I enjoyed three quiet days to myself and then the phone rang.

'Hi, T, it's me.' Shane sounded sad.

'Are you all right?'

'I miss you,' he said. 'You'll wait for me, won't you?' He sounded insecure. 'I'm going to turn my life around, but you'll still be there?'

'Yeah, I said I would,' I sighed.

He'd turned himself into the police, so he must be serious this time, I thought. He must really love me. I couldn't abandon him now.

'So do you think you could send me some money?' He brought the conversation back down to earth with a bump.

'What do you need money for?' I asked.

'To buy tuna. I need my protein to build more muscle; I can't survive on this prison food crap. We get to put through a shopping list on Monday which arrives on Thursday,' he explained.

'Sounds more like a hotel than a prison,' I scoffed.

'I'm going to get my body looking even bigger for you.'

That was the last thing I wanted, an even bigger Shane smacking me around.

'So, you gonna send me money?'

I barely had enough money to feed myself and my kids, how was I going to manage?

'How much do you want?' I asked.

'Thirty pounds,' he said.

He could tell I was wavering so he turned on the guilt trip.

'It's your fault I'm in here,' he attacked.

'What?'

'You didn't get the GBH charges dropped and now there are four more against me because you reported all that stuff over Christmas.'

He was right, it *was* my fault. He would never have done all those things if I hadn't provoked him.

'OK, I'll send you the money,' I mumbled, like I'd been told off by my teacher.

'I love you, T,' he reminded me.

'I know, I love you too,' I told him.

Money was going to be tight for a while but I was just going to have to make do. It was the least I could do to make it up to Shane for opening my mouth. But as soon as I'd put the cash in the post he was asking me for the next favour – to get the police to drop the charges.

'I can't, Shane, I told you, it's out of my hands,' I pleaded.

'Well, try harder,' he snapped.

'There's nothing I can do, what can I do?'

The line went silent.

'Shane?'

Nothing.

'Please, Shane.' I needed to know he wasn't mad at me. I always crumbled when he ignored me.

'Well, you're going to have to keep your mouth shut in court then,' he finally said.

'What?' I gasped.

'Yes,' he replied, like he'd asked me to make him a cup of tea.

'No way,' I insisted. I couldn't do that.

'You got me into this mess; you get me out of it,' Shane said, losing his temper. He hung up on me and I was left hanging. I couldn't breathe. I put my hand onto my chest and felt my galloping heart beneath my fingers.

What was I going to do? If I knew Shane, he wouldn't give up on this idea, he never did when he got something in his head. I was trapped between a rock and a hard place but I knew that if I didn't do as he said he would punish me when he got out. So much for my rest. I was just as much a nervous wreck now Shane was in prison. He was calling me nearly every day, so I wasn't getting any time off. And if he wasn't calling, he was sending me letters telling me how much he loved me.

A card arrived for me in the post at the end of the week.

'I love you' was scrawled in swirly handwriting above a picture of a teddy bear clutching a bunch of flowers. Inside, Shane told me he was going to send me a different card every week with his canteen money. My heart melted, it was such a romantic gesture – he must really love me.

I couldn't wait to tell him thank-you for the card, but his mood had changed again when he called later that evening.

'You've got to get me out of here.' His voice was panicky.

'What? What's wrong?' I asked.

'I went into the other wing today and that's when this guy saw me,' he rambled.

'Who?' I was confused.

'Someone who thinks I grassed him up to the cops for some shit that went down in my pass house. There were loads of them standing around when he called me a grass,' he explained, his voice trembling.

'Is he going to kill you?' I screeched.

'Look, if someone comes after me, I'm just going to do what I have to do to survive.' He was playing the hard guy.

'You're scaring me, Shane,' I said. This violent underworld was so foreign to me I didn't know what to think. 'Are you going to be OK?' I imagined some big guy in a vest and prison trousers coming up behind Shane and knifing him in the back.

'You've got to get me out of here, Tina,' he insisted. He was emotionally blackmailing me, although I was too scared to see it.

I played for time, 'OK, I'll help you.'

'Good girl,' he said. I could almost hear him smile.

A few days later another card arrived for me with 'You're Special' on the front. Inside he asked if I was missing him. How could he ask that? I didn't have the chance to miss him; he was in touch every day. Shane made me believe he was pining for me and that he really was going to change, which filled me with hope.

I rubbed my bleary eyes. I hadn't slept a wink since Shane had told me his life was in danger. I'd been having nightmares about him getting his throat slit but last night's was the worst. I dreamed that a gang had charged into his cell while he was sleeping and pinned him down while one of them gouged out his eyes. I woke up screaming, just as the blood spurted everywhere. My adrenalin was pumping so hard I couldn't get back to sleep, so I got up and checked on the boys. They looked so peaceful and I wished I could be young again. How did my life get so messed up?

Shane called me again that evening to drum it into me that it was life or death that I get him out of there.

He said the trial date, that was set for 14 February, had been adjourned while more evidence was gathered, so he wasn't coming out any time soon.

'You'll wait for me, won't you?' he kept asking.

'Yeah, I said I would,' I kept replying.

I should have felt like I finally had the upper hand – he was inside, begging me to wait for him – but somehow I was still under his control. I stayed in my house waiting for his phone calls. I didn't use my new-found freedom to see my friends and family; instead I spent my evenings at home writing him eight-page letters about what I'd been doing, and what we would do together when he got out of prison.

'Mummy, Mummy, where's Shane?' Liam asked.

'And Liam says he misses you,' I scribbled in my letter. I took a deep breath as that nearly brought a tear to my eye. 'I want us to be a family,' I wrote to Shane. I told him about my dreams of us going on holiday together and that I would even move to Manchester to live if that's what he wanted. 'I know you like it there, we can make a new life for ourselves, you can get a job.' I was bursting with ideas. 'I miss you, I love you,' I signed off. Sometimes my letters were so long they would take three days to write, but I needed to tell him everything that I was doing. I felt lucky that I had someone who paid me all that attention, and I needed to show him how grateful I was.

Before I knew it a month had slipped by without Shane. I missed him more than ever but, for the first time in over a year, I felt strong, because I finally had the space to breathe. I didn't have to worry about the cops raiding my house, social services turning up. I could relax. The only thing I had to worry about was the looming court appearance, but that wasn't until 10 March. When Shane broke the news that he would be staying in prison until then, now that all five charges were going to be heard on the same day, I felt relief. I had another month to myself.

I could tell Shane knew I was getting stronger from the way he sounded bitter on the phone. He didn't like to hear about the things I was doing. He'd rather talk about himself and the danger he was in. I started keeping secrets so as not to upset him. I didn't tell him Lorraine was stopping by in the mornings again, or about our family trips to the local pub for a roast dinner on Sundays. I didn't tell him that I was going to go clubbing in Penzance with my brother Paul and my friend Wendy – he would have lost it with jealousy.

Bit by bit I was getting my confidence back. I'd had my hair and nails done and spent a morning shopping for a new outfit.

'You look all right, Tina,' I said to my reflection. The bags under my eyes had vanished; my skin was looking clear and dewy, my blue eyes were sparkling.

I zipped open my make-up bag and pulled out my sparkling eye shadows. How do you do this again? It had been so long since I'd got ready for a night out. I brought out my baby blues with silver sparkles and lots of black eyeliner. I dabbed my favourite pink gloss along my lips, and slipped into my brand new pair of heels. I took one last look in the mirror, grabbed my handbag and headed to the taxi waiting outside.

Two steps out of my door I felt sick with nerves. I felt guilty for having fun while Shane was in prison, because of me. He would be so angry if he saw me now. My knees buckled with fear. I remembered the feeling of his fist on my face and I edged backwards to the safety of my house. The sick feeling was growing in my stomach and I clasped my mouth to stop myself retching.

'Beep-beep,' the taxi driver tooted.

I can't do it, he'll hate me for it.

My phone started ringing – it was my brother Paul.

'Where are you?' he said. I could barely hear him above the rowdy bar noise.

I was just about to let him down when Wendy came walking along the street to meet me.

'Wow, check you out!' she gasped, looking me up and down. 'Those shoes are wicked.'

'I'm not feeling too good,' I mumbled, like a kid trying to get a sick day off school. That's what Shane had reduced me to – someone who grovelled. I think Wendy, like the rest of my family and friends, knew the real reason I was afraid to leave the house.

'There is no way you're not going out when you look as stunning as that,' she said, linking my arm and dragging me into the taxi.

She was right; I deserved a night out, and the old Tina blossomed from within.

'We're on our way,' I told Paul.

I laughed, I danced, I caught up with old friends – I remembered how much fun I used to have before Shane came into my life. I had people coming up to me all night, telling me how they'd been afraid to even say hello when I was with Shane. Word had got about that he was in the nick and suddenly horror stories were coming out of the woodwork.

'He's a psycho, he stabbed his dog to death when he'd had enough of him,' one of Shane's so-called friends revealed.

'What?' I gasped.

'Yeah, his Rottweiler,' he said, as if everyone knew.

Another person who lived on my estate said they had seen Shane spying on me while I was in my garden.

My head was spinning; I didn't know what to believe. But before I had time to digest it, Shane was on the phone, getting back inside my head.

'I'm a dead man in here!' he shouted. 'You're the reason I'm in here. You've gotta get me out.' He scared me. It was like he knew I'd got away for the evening and he needed to rein me in.

'I'll fix it,' I said, and felt sick with guilt.

'You'd better fucking fix it,' he threatened. 'It's a set-up, the police have set me up,' he ranted.

Nothing was ever Shane's fault; he thought everyone was against him; he thought he was a renegade just like Raoul Moat.

'And you'd better not be spending time with your whore of a sister, Lorraine,' he warned, twisting the knife. He was always trying to turn me against my family.

'That's my sister you're talking about,' I mumbled.

'She's a fucking slut.'

It was pointless talking to him when he was in one of his moods. I just had to sit there and take it. It was my fault he was there, he was allowed to be angry at me.

'I love you. I'll speak to you tomorrow,' I grovelled.

But every time he knocked me down it was taking me less time to get back on my feet. The next day I borrowed Lorraine's computer so I could get some ideas to redecorate. Shane had destroyed my house, so it was time to reclaim it.

'What do you think about this kitchen?' I asked Ben, showing him a few designs.

'Can we have one of those fridges that have an icemaker?' he asked.

'You *would* want one of those,' I joked, and ruffled his hair.

I was determined to make my place look like a show home. I'd been sleeping on just a mattress for over a year, and enough was enough. I bought a black gothic-style metal-framed double bed for the bedroom off a friend. I had a new kitchen fitted, a new cream carpet laid down in the front room, and I painted the walls a matching sandstone colour. I left one wall free, which I painted roasted red, and that's where I mounted my new plasma TV.

'It looks amazing, Tine,' said Lorraine, opening and closing all my new units in the kitchen.

'I'm so proud of you, sis.' She hugged me.

'What for, girl?'

'For doing all this,' she said, raising her arms to the room. 'And for getting Shane out of your life,' she added.

I couldn't bring myself to tell her I was still speaking to him almost every day.

'How are you feeling about court? Do you want me to come with you?' She squeezed my arm.

'Just something I've got to get on with,' I said with a shrug. 'Yeah, I would like it if you could be there.'

The trial was only days away now, but I still didn't know what I was going to do. The police had told me if Shane was found guilty then he'd only be in prison for a few more weeks because he'd already served his sentence in the time leading up to it. So what was the point of risking my life for a few weeks? It hurt to think about it.

'I should take some pictures of my new house,' I said, changing the subject. I pulled out my phone camera and started snapping away. If there was one thing I had learned to do well since meeting Shane, it was sticking my head in the sand. If I didn't talk about it, it wasn't real.

'It's Thursday that I'm taking us to Truro Crown Court?' Lorraine confirmed.

'Yes,' I replied reluctantly.

'You're going to be fine; he needs to pay for what he did to you.'

'I know.'

I bowed my head.

I had my second pep talk of the week the following morning when two cops turned up at my door. I recognised the lady; she had questioned me during the lead-up to Shane being put on tag.

'Hi, Tina, I'm Lara Pimm, and this is my colleague Mike. We work with the domestic violence unit.' She shook my hand. She had long, dark, chestnut-coloured hair, a curvy, womanly body and a smile that could light up a room. I felt that I could trust her.

'Wow, your house is looking amazing,' she gasped.

'Oh yeah, the last time you saw it everything was smashed up, wasn't it?' I realised. 'Let me show you what I've done,' I said as I proudly led her around.

'You're looking really well,' Lara kept saying.

'I feel much better,' I agreed.

'And we need to keep Shane out of your life.' Her voice turned stern.

'Yeah, I know,' I lied. 'Would you like a cup of tea?'

I led them into my new kitchen. I backed into the corner and waited for the lecture.

'So you know Shane is in court this Thursday?' Lara started.

'Yes.'

I poured the boiling water into the mugs.

'Are you going to be there?'

'Yeah, I'll be there.'

'So he's being tried for the original GBH from last April and four further counts of criminal damage to your property and assaults made over the Christmas period,' she reminded me. 'Are you ready?' Her voice was now warm and caring.

'Yeah,' I lied again.

She looked at me with concerned eyes.

'I'm OK, don't worry, I'm going to get up there and tell the truth,' I said.

'It's going to be all right, Tina, you have us for support. Do you want me to take you there?'

'No, it's OK, my sister will drive me.' I couldn't look her in the eye. She was being caring and I was as guilty as Shane.

I was in turmoil. I knew what I *should* do, but I didn't know if I could do it. I weighed up the options. I didn't know what to do. If I grassed Shane up he'd be out in weeks anyway, and then he'd come for me – he'd kill me. I had to protect myself.

I was on tenterhooks all day Wednesday, waiting for the call.

'Just ring and put me out of my misery,' I shouted at my phone.

I sat on the edge of my seat, my hands clasped between my knees. Finally my mobile sang.

'So, are you going to be in court tomorrow, then?' Shane began.

'Yes,' I said, like an obedient dog.

'You're going to mess up, I know you will?' he growled.

'So, what are you going to say?' he prodded.

'We've been through this, Shane,' I pleaded.

I was frightened and told him what he wanted to hear. Shane had pleaded guilty to the other charges, but the GBH was the one he cared about because it was the most serious.

'I love you. I can't wait until we're together again,' Shane said, softening.

'I love you too, see you tomorrow.' I choked on the words.

It had been nearly two and half months since I had seen him. I was excited and sad at the same time. I couldn't wait to feel his arms around me but I was terrified of things going back to how they were, especially as I'd just got my life back on track.

I tossed and turned all night long, my mind whirring with anxious thoughts.

Oh God, he's going to be waiting for me in that courtroom; I can feel his eyes on me already.

16

Day of Reckoning

I sat at the edge of my bed, delaying getting dressed for a few minutes longer.

I slowly rolled my jeans up each leg like I was carefully putting on a pair of tights. I stood up on my shaky legs and reached for my white vest and black cardigan, which I had laid out the night before. I slipped my feet into my black Ugg boots and played with my hair in the front of the mirror.

Up? Down? Down, I decided. It wasn't about looking smart for court; I was making an effort for Shane.

My stomach lurched as I thought about seeing him in the dock.

I poured myself a bowl of cereal but after one mouthful I felt I was going to be sick. I pushed it to one side and lit a cigarette instead. With every nervous puff, I went through in my mind what was going to happen in court.

My stomach lurched again.

Lorraine was early picking me up but I was glad of the company.

'You all set?' she asked.

'Yeah.'

Lorraine could tell something was up as she was deep in thought the whole journey there. She hated Shane but she understood what I was going through because she had been there from the start of our relationship.

'How're you feeling about seeing him?' she asked, breaking the silence.

'Scared.'

Scared he would come after me.

'You'll be fine, just say your piece and then get out of there,' Lorraine said, as she drove through the car park looking for a space.

I took another deep breath and let her lead the way into Truro Crown Court. We were met by a lady officer, who introduced herself as PC Ferguson. She took us through a side door, the clip-clop of her heels echoing along the corridor.

'Wait in here,' she said, as she ushered us into the witness protection room.

It was small and airless and smelled of panic from the hundreds of witnesses who had sat here before me. I clasped my hands together to stop them shaking. I couldn't look at Lorraine.

What was going to happen in court? What was I going to do?

I rummaged through my handbag and pulled out a piece of chewing gum.

'It's time.' PC Ferguson beckoned me through the ancient wooden door. I looked to Lorraine for reassurance and she flashed me a sympathetic smile.

The room was massive and eerily quiet except for the sound of people coughing and shuffling through paper. I could feel everyone's eyes watching me as I walked nervously to the witness stand. I could feel *his* eyes on me. I looked to my left and our eyes locked and then he turned his head away.

My stomach felt like it had dropped through my body. Shane was sat behind a glass panel. His head was completely shaved for the first time ever. I just had to look at him and all the feelings came flooding back.

'Miss Nash,' the clerk said, trying to catch my attention.

'Oh, sorry,' I muttered. I was a million miles away. On a tropical island lying in Shane's arms.

The clerk held out the Bible and told me to put my hand on it and repeat after him.

'I, Tina Nash, swear to tell the truth, the whole truth, and nothing but the truth, so help me God.'

I steadied myself by clasping on to the wooden shelf around the inside of the box. I didn't even notice I was digging my nails in, I was so tense. My barrister stood up and prompted me into retelling what had happened on the night of 27 April 2010.

'Is it correct that you were in your bedroom when Mr Jenkin first attacked you by punching you in the face?' he said in his plummy voice.

My heart was galloping so fast, trapping the words in my throat.

'No . . .' I began. I cleared my throat. 'No, I exaggerated everything because I was angry and jealous.'

My barrister's face dropped.

'Is it not true, Miss Nash, that Mr Jenkin hit you several times in the face and then tried to gouge your eyes out before throwing you down the stairs?'

I started chewing my gum vigorously. I looked to Shane but he wouldn't look at me.

'He didn't lay a finger on me,' I said.

I looked across to Lorraine and she shook her head with disappointment.

'I made it up, I fell down the stairs,' I kept going.

'How exactly did you *fall* down the stairs, Miss Nash?' The barrister wouldn't let it go.

'Shane was bringing his stuff out and his bag caught me,' I stuttered, pulse sky-high. Beads of sweat were dribbling down my back.

I was only on the stand for fifteen minutes. I was asked to step down and PC Ferguson shot me a look of disgust as she led me back into the small room. I sat down on the hard chair and stared into space. There was no way I could look at her – I felt guilty enough as it was. The loud sound of the ticking clock was my only friend as I waited for what was going to happen next.

An hour later PC Ferguson returned and broke the silence. 'The judge wants to see you.'

'Me?' I put my hands over my chest.

She held open the door and I shuffled back into the high-ceilinged courtroom. Shane wasn't there this time, neither was the jury, or Lorraine. It was just me, the two barristers and the judge. I stood before him, shaking, like I was back in school being told off by the headmaster. He told me that he didn't believe I was telling the truth.

'But,' he paused, 'there is nothing we can do about it.'

I bowed my head in shame.

'You've said what you've had to say,' he said, then paused again as he waited to catch my attention. 'I just hope this doesn't come back to haunt you.' He looked me right in the eye. His words were like lightning striking through my heart.

'Yes, Your Honour,' I mumbled. I turned and followed PC Ferguson out of the courtroom.

'What happens now?' I asked her. I wanted to get as far away as possible.

'We have to wait for how the judge decides to sentence Jenkin for the other charges. He'll probably be out today,' she sighed.

My stomach lurched again at the thought of seeing him in just a matter of hours, although I was surprised there was anything left of it after the number of somersaults it had turned that day. There was an awkward silence as PC Ferguson looked me up and down.

'I don't believe what you've said,' she started.

My eyes shot to the ground again, as I was handed my second scolding.

'I understand why you did it but it doesn't make it any easier for us, because a lot of man-hours went into getting him convicted.'

I nodded, like a little girl being told off.

'I hope you can live with your decision,' she warned.

I just prayed the judge and the cop would be wrong.

'OK,' I mumbled, and sidled out of the door to face scolding number three – from Lorraine. But my sister didn't have any words for me. She just curled her lips into her mouth to express her indignation.

'I'll get us a cup of tea,' I said, backing off to the drinks machine. I was sinking in a quicksand of guilt and needed some space to breathe.

Lorraine may have hated me for what I did, but she stuck by me for all those hours we waited in the hall for Shane to be released. She barely said a word but I knew she still loved me.

'He's registered his new address to my house,' I revealed.

'OK, I'll drop you both back there,' she said with pity in her eyes. She knew there was nothing she could do to pull me away from him. That it had to run its course.

Although I felt guilty, I also felt an incredible weight lifted off my shoulders. The whole time Shane had been in prison I'd believed it was my entire fault. Now I didn't owe him anything. I just hoped he wouldn't break his promise.

'It's going to be different this time,' I told Lorraine. 'He's promised he's going to get a job, start his life again.'

'He ain't ever going to change, Tina,' Lorraine said, shaking her head in despair.

Just as I was about to reply, a door creaked open and Shane appeared. He strutted his way down the length of the hall wearing a big Cheshire cat grin and carrying his possessions in a see-through bag with 'HMP' stamped across it.

My heart was in my mouth. I was like a love-struck teenager again.

'Hey, baby,' he said, wrapping his giant arms around me. He leaned forward and planted a long lingering kiss on my lips. His mouth was warm and moist, re-igniting all those old feelings of lust and love.

'Ahem.' Lorraine cleared her throat.

'All right, Lorraine,' Shane greeted my sister. She flashed him a sarcastic smile and then told us it was time to get going. Shane couldn't keep his hands off me as we walked to the car park. He had lost a bit of weight and he smelled strange; he reeked of prison.

'I can't believe they let you out today,' I said.

'That's because you stood up for me,' he said, and nuzzled my neck.

I felt sick. I hated myself and I never wanted to be reminded of it again. It was one of the many bad memories I was going to lock away. We were looking to the future now. He promised me a new Shane, a fresh start.

'What do you want to do tonight?' I asked.

'I don't care, just as long as it's with you,' he said, and squeezed my hand tightly.

He's changed, he's changed, I can feel it in my heart.

Lorraine chauffeured us back to my house; she didn't say a word but rolled her eyes at almost everything that came out of Shane's mouth. I couldn't wait to open my front door and show him what I had done to the place – for our new life together. My heart was jumping with happiness as I turned the key in the door. I grinned at Shane, who was none the wiser.

'What?' he shrugged.

'Tadaaaa!' I exclaimed, welcoming him into our new home.

His eyes lit up like those of a kid in a sweet store.

'Oh my God, it looks like a five-star hotel in here compared to prison.'

'So you like it?' I asked, beaming.

'I love it, and I love you.' He lifted me up into his arms.

Lorraine turned away in disgust and I wriggled free so as not to upset her.

'I've been trying to sort my life out too while you've been away,' I told him. I wanted him to know I'd been the dutiful girlfriend, staying at home fixing things. Lorraine couldn't watch us together any longer and told me she would check on me the next day.

'OK, girl.' I hoped she would forgive me one day.

As soon as she left the feeling of being alone hit me like a bus. It was just me and Shane now. I'd made my bed and now I had to lie in it. There was no going back, no going crying to my family or the police, I just had to hope that Shane didn't let me down, that the judge's words didn't come true.

'Why don't we celebrate by getting a takeaway?' I suggested.

We headed to the local kebab shop and came back with a small feast of kebabs, pizza, beer and cider, which Shane paid for. He was opening doors for me, holding my hand; he was making a special effort to impress. He even let me choose what DVD we watched.

'Liam's been missing you, we've all missed you,' I said, snuggling into him.

'Yeah, I can't wait to see the boys,' he replied, and kissed my forehead.

More than anything I wanted us to be a family and he was showing all the signs of a changed man who wanted to care for us. I lost count of how many times we made love that night.

'I love you,' he said, as he moved his powerful body gently inside me.

'I love you too.' I looked into his dark eyes.

17

Too Good to Be True

'I'm sorry. Shane, I'm sorry, I didn't mean it, I'm sorry.' I cowered on the kitchen floor with my arms over my face.

Less than a week had gone by, and Shane had already shattered our dreams. We'd been bickering in the kitchen and then he'd pushed me to the ground as punishment. I lay with my legs in a tangled mess thinking, God, things haven't changed at all.

'You fucking bitch,' he shouted. He might as well have spat on me while I lay there.

He then puffed out his chest and smashed his beer bottle against the wall, raining glass and booze down on me.

Oh God, he's coming for me.

A shard of glass landed by my hand and I grabbed it in self-defence. I was terrified, and I was furious at him for breaking our happy ending. I'd had enough. The fighter in me forced me up onto my feet and I looked at him with hatred.

'Do you want me to finish myself off?' I snapped. I held the shard to my throat in desperation. 'Do you want me to make it easier for you?' I squeezed the glass so tightly the edges bit into my hand.

His snarl turned into a smirk and I hated him even more.

I'm going to smash this glass in your face, that'll wipe that smirk away.

I wanted to do it so badly but I knew if I did, he would finish me off.

Shane lurched forward and wrapped his big arm around my neck like a boa constrictor. I scratched at his skin but he squeezed harder and my head became light and floaty. He squeezed even harder and I dropped the glass to the floor. He took the air out of me one last time and then released me from his grip. I dropped like a bag of bones. He leered down at me like I was a piece of shit and then walked into the other room, leaving me to pick up the pieces. I cradled my bruised neck, wishing the ground would swallow me up.

You stupid idiot, Tina, why did you take him back? You stupid, stupid idiot.

The words floated in the tears in my eyes, as I realised there was no escape.

I had to go up to my room and lie down because he'd squeezed every last bit of energy out of me. I lay there and imagined I was floating . . . above my broken body, above everything, I was light and soaring and a million miles away from my problems.

I was woken by the sound of someone banging on my front door. I rubbed my aching neck as I staggered down the stairs to see who it was. Shane was already there – waiting for me. He stood with his arms crossed, guarding the door like a nightclub bouncer.

'Tina,' my friend Wendy called through the letter box.

Shane held his finger up to his lips, warning me to keep my mouth shut. I stood still like an obedient dog, as I waited for my friend, my lifeline, to go.

'Look at the state of you,' he said, pointing to my neck once the coast was clear. 'Can't have anyone seeing you like that.' He shook his head as if it was my fault.

My heart bolted to my throat when I saw the bruises in the mirror. It was worse than the last time he'd punished me. I had a thick purple band that reached as high as my jaw. If social services saw me like this they would definitely take Ben and Liam from me. I'd fought so hard to keep them and now he was gambling it all away again. I looked at him with pleading eyes but they didn't make a dent in his steel composure. His face was devoid of all emotion. He turned like a robot and started drawing the curtains in the front room.

'What are you doing?' I whimpered.

'Don't want the Old Bill round, do I?' he said, walking up the staircase to finish the job upstairs.

Ben and Liam's room faced the back garden, so Shane didn't mind them having their light on at night, but I had to creep around the house with just a candle and blow it out whenever Shane heard a noise.

I was now his prisoner. I had to follow his rules or he would punish me.

Wendy came knocking for me again the next day. I'd seen her and Lorraine almost every day for the two and a half months that Shane was in prison, so she knew something was wrong.

'TINA!' she yelled for the fifth time. I had to tuck my hands under my armpits to stop myself reaching for the door.

'TINA!' she called again.

Shane's face was getting angrier by the minute.

Please, Wendy, leave me alone.

'Tina, open up,' she demanded, banging again. I had to do something or Shane was going to go nuts on me.

I ran upstairs and knocked on Ben's door.

'Hi, Ben, sweetheart, could you do a favour for Mummy?' I asked tentatively. I was desperate.

'What?' he sulked. He knew Shane was making me unhappy.

'Can you please go downstairs and tell Wendy that I have a sinus infection.'

He shot me a knowing look that went straight to my heart.

'Please, Ben,' I begged.

'OK, Mum, I'll do it,' he grumped.

'Good boy.' I ruffled his silky hair as he passed by me.

I stood at the top of the stairs shaking as I listened to my son lie for me.

'Where's your mum, Ben?' Wendy's voice sounded urgent and worried.

'Mum's not very well, she's upstairs suffering from a sinus infection,' he mumbled.

There was a long pause and then Wendy said I needed to look after myself. I let out a deep sigh of relief and went downstairs to check if Shane was happy with me. I felt like I was walking on eggshells, terrified I might upset him at any moment. I peered into the front room and he was back playing his bloody video games.

'Thank you, Ben,' I said, folding my arms around my boy. 'Shane doesn't want anyone coming around here for a little while,' was my pathetic explanation.

Poor Ben didn't know what to say; he just stared at me with his big eyes.

'It's just for a few days.' I pinched my hand to stop myself crying. I had to be strong for my boys.

'I'm going to the shops later, what would you like?' I asked him, changing the subject.

'I dunno, crisps,' Ben said, grinning. He was a typical teenager who liked his junk food.

'I'll see what I can do,' I said, and winked at him.

I had to wait until dark before going to the local shops so no one would see me. I wrapped a thick winter scarf around my neck to hide the bruises before stepping out into the warm March evening. I hunched my shoulders forward and strode quickly down the street, wishing I was invisible. I was a shadow of my old self – confident fun-loving Tina had shrunk to a seven-stone jittery wreck.

I walked like a robot through the aisles of the shop, turning my whole body with my head so no one would see my bruises.

'Haven't seen you in a while, Nash,' said the friendly shopkeeper.

'Yeah,' I replied, not wanting to enter into any chitchat. I just had to get my essentials and leave. Shane would be waiting for me, counting the minutes until I got home. Everything seemed normal when I let myself in – Shane was calm and acting like nothing had happened. I knew I was back riding the honeymoon wave where things would be magical for a week or so, but I couldn't pretend any longer.

I'd had my taste of freedom and I longed for it back. I just didn't know how to get it back. Instead I withdrew into myself and became as quiet as a mouse, only speaking when asked a question. I'd sit on the kitchen counter by the back door, staring out at the street while I puffed away on a cigarette. Shane hated not knowing what I was thinking. He could tell I'd had enough and I was slipping away from him.

'I can tell you don't want to be with me any more,' he said, watching me from the doorway. His presence was suffocating.

I inhaled deeply, taking in my thoughts. I couldn't say, 'No I don't,' but my expression must have given me away. He pulled his fist back and came looming right up to my face. His mouth was twisted like he was going to go for me.

'Sorry, Shane, sorry, I was just joking, sorry.' I covered my head with my arms.

He stopped and pulled back, giving me another chance. He stared at me with his black eyes. I looked to the ground like a naughty girl and he lunged for me, his fist millimetres from my cheek.

'Sorry, Shane, sorry,' I apologised again, even though I hadn't said anything.

He backed off and watched me again and then lunged again. He must have made me cower in the corner at least seven times before he finally gave up. I learned something though – if I begged enough it made him stop. I banked the information for my future beatings.

Shane was happy that I'd kept Lorraine away for a couple of weeks by faking a painful tooth abscess, but now the bruises around my neck had finally faded, I had less of a reason to hide from the world. It was then that the penny dropped – I realised Shane wasn't worried about the cops seeing his handiwork; he was hurting me so he could have me all to himself.

*   *   *

'Lorraine keeps calling me,' I announced, as her name flashed up on my mobile again. I was too scared to ask if I could see her.

'So what?' Shane spat.

I didn't dare plead with him; instead, I took myself away to my sanctuary in the kitchen and stared out the window, longing for my freedom back.

'T, can you come in here and help me wire these speakers up?' Shane asked.

It was good to keep busy, it kept my mind off the things I was missing. I walked into the front room to find him bent double trying to wire my equipment up to his stereo. Thanks to my DJ work, this was one area I did know about, a chance for me to impress him, make him love me.

'Let me have a go.' I accepted the challenge and started tinkering with the wires. He kept a close eye on me, watching every move I made.

'Yes, I think I've got it,' I said proudly. But I was so nervous my hand caught on a lead as I was celebrating. I watched in slow motion as his stereo fell from the shelf to the floor.

CRASH!

'Oh my God, I'm sorry, I'm so sorry, I'm so sorry,' I apologised, cradling the stereo like it was a baby.

He took it out of my hands and silently inspected it for damage while I held my breath.

'I'm so sorry, I'm so sorry,' I said, like I was begging for my life.

He shrugged and told me it looked like it was OK. He wasn't mad with me. My heart sang – I was going to be all right.

'Oh, thank God,' I said, trembling. 'I can be so clumsy.'

Shane sat back down on the sofa and put his feet up. It looked like our honeymoon could go into next week with the way he was behaving. I hung around for a short while longer to make doubly sure he was still happy with me before making a cup of tea.

'Would you like a brew?' I called out. But there was no reason to shout – Shane was right behind me. I hadn't heard his footsteps. His face was the most twisted I'd ever seen it. He wound his fist back and punched me in the head.

SMACK!

The force sent me flying from the doorway of my kitchen into my downstairs bathroom.

SMACK!

I bashed my head on the wall before falling to the ground.

I felt a warm, wet sensation flow over my face and then the river of blood covered my clothes and the bathroom floor. There was so much blood I thought I was dying. I reached my shaky hands to the pain in my forehead and felt a gaping hole that turned my fingers crimson.

Shane was just staring at me, not saying a word.

I reached out my blood-soaked hands for his help.

He just stared at me.

I dropped them limply back to my side. I was going to have to do this by myself. I dug deep and found the strength to pull my body up by clinging on to the bath. The whole time his eyes were watching me, enjoying my suffering. I clung to the wall and then turned to face him. I felt another warm, wet sensation, but this time in my jeans.

'Oh my God, I'm weeing myself,' I cried. 'I can't make it stop.'

I stood helplessly in a puddle of piss and blood while Shane shook his head with disgust. He turned and walked away, while I was left stripped of all my dignity.

My head felt like someone had put an axe through it. The bleeding was so bad I couldn't make out how serious the damage was. I washed my body clean but I deliberately left my face smeared and stained with blood. I wanted him to wake up in the morning and see what he had done to me this time. I staggered to bed dizzy from the pain and loss of blood and I passed out as soon as my head hit the pillow.

I kept waking up in feverish sweats and then passing out again. At one point I dreamed I was lying on my trampoline in the sunshine because I felt so hot. I'd wake up feeling happy and then the pain would knock me out. The fever was so bad by the morning that my skin felt like it was crawling with insects. I rolled over to find Shane staring at me as if he'd been watching me for hours.

'Look at the state of you, go and clean yourself up,' he sneered, showing no remorse.

I knotted my hand around the side of the bed and pulled my broken body off it. I staggered to the bathroom downstairs, just like I had done so many times before. My face looked like something from a horror film. I was covered in dry crusty blood and there was an inch-long gash across my forehead where you could see my skull.

'Oh my God,' I whispered in disbelief. I needed help.

I used the banister to pull myself back up to my bedroom and leaned on my door frame while I pleaded with Shane.

'I need to go to hospital,' I said, pointing to the hole in my head.

'You'll be fine,' he said.

'I really think I need stitches,' I asked again.

No answer. There was no way he was letting me go now. I rolled back down on the bed and thought about my sister Lorraine's words – 'He's going to kill you'.

He's going to kill me, he's going to kill me, I sang in my head, as I drifted off again.

I woke from my feverish nap to the sound of grunting coming from downstairs. All the curtains were closed as I tiptoed my way to the front room.

'Arrrrrgh!' Shane bellowed, as he lifted his weights up to his chest. I'd never seen so many weights on a bar in my life; the discs were so huge the bar was bending. Sweat was dripping off his tattooed body and his veins looked like they were going to burst open with the pressure. No wonder he'd cut my head open with just one punch. I quivered.

He looked like a snorting bull as he caught his breath between lifts. He saw me watching and puffed out his chest like a gorilla before reaching for the bar again.

'Arrrrgh!' he hollered, as he punched out another ten reps.

I couldn't watch; everything I had first loved about him – his big protective body – I now feared. I escaped into the kitchen to my hiding spot by the window and before I knew it he was standing at the door, grinning.

He cocked his head to the side as if he was surveying the damage.

'You look like you've been shot in the head,' he said. His eyes were crazy and full of testosterone. He then lifted his hand into the shape of a gun.

'Peeeew!' He pretended to shoot me and then roared with laughter.

My lip quivered as I felt the tears coming. He kept watching me, expecting me to say something, but I had no words left. He walked up to my side and my body froze with fear. I could smell the sweat and heat coming off him.

'You don't love me any more, do you?' he said with a crazed expression.

I was too afraid to speak this time.

'Do you?' he repeated, pulling his fist back.

'I'm sorry, Shane, I'm sorry. It's my fault, I'm sorry,' I cried. 'I do love you, I'm sorry.'

He backed off when he heard those words and then looked at me with his sad eyes. He was like Frankenstein – a monster who didn't really want to be one, only he didn't know how to be anything else. I knew there was still some good left in him but I just couldn't be the one to save him any more.

My new injuries meant I was back in hiding. Liam was too little to notice our house had turned into a dungeon, but Ben spent his evenings locked away in his room watching TV. Wendy kept calling round for me, my sister kept ringing, and I kept playing the sick card to keep them away. My days were spent looking after my boys and looking up at the sky from my trampoline, dreaming of a better life.

The weather turned out to be my only saviour, as it was unusually hot for mid-April. I lay on my trampoline all week while Shane watched me from the front room. A hundred questions whirred through my mind but there was one that I kept chewing over. It was something one of Shane's friends had said to me while he was banged up.

'Shane,' I asked tentatively.

'Yeah.' He didn't look up from his computer game.

'You know that dog you used to have, your Rottweiler?' I started.

'Yeah,' he grunted, and carried on killing zombies.

'Is it true that you stabbed it to death?' I had to know.

He paused for a moment.

'Yeah, it's true. So?'

I was speechless.

18

He Took My Eyes

I covered my face with my hands and screamed.

'I don't like this.'

Shane couldn't tear his eyes away from the sick images of a Chinese girl getting her eye gouged out by a psychopath in the horror film *Hostel*.

'This ain't right,' I said as I cowered into his excited body.

He ignored my pleas and I was forced to carry on watching the DVD until the end. It brought back all the memories of when Shane had tried to take my eyes out almost exactly a year ago to the day.

I skipped from one nightmare to the next that night. I dreamed I was strapped to the chair like the Chinese girl in the film, and Shane was the psychopath holding a buzzing drill to my face. I then dreamed of Shane stabbing his poor dog to death.

'No, Shane, no,' I yelled, as I sat bolt upright in bed. The sheets were so wet with sweat you could have wrung them out. I looked across and Shane was sleeping like a baby. He was like Teflon, nothing seemed to touch him. I couldn't stay in that dark room a second longer, so I sprang out of bed and crept downstairs to have a quiet cigarette alone.

Dawn had become my favourite time of the day because I knew Shane wouldn't come looking for me. I could watch the sun rising and hope that today was going to be different, that today I wouldn't be scared any more. Ben was the first to come down the stairs and I made him a cup of tea and breakfast while he rubbed his sleepy eyes.

'Go and have a shower, love, or you'll be late for school,' I nagged. I was trying my best to make everything seem normal.

Today was going to be different though, because Shane had to go to his community service, which meant my prison doors would be open for a few hours. I would finally be able to see my sister Lorraine after weeks in hiding.

I was sunbathing on my trampoline when she came knocking. I'd forgotten about the gash on my head but Lorraine nearly fell backwards when she saw the hole.

'What the bloody hell has happened to you?' she shrieked.

'Oh,' I said, touching my wound. It had been three weeks but it hadn't healed properly because I wasn't allowed to go to hospital for stitches. I had to think on my feet and make up a lie.

'I hit my head.'

'What do you mean, you hit your head?' Lorraine asked as she inspected it sceptically.

My heart started to race again like it had when I was lying in court.

'I was bending down to pick something up in the kitchen and I hit my head on the cupboard door when I stood up,' I lied.

Lorraine stared at me quizzically.

'I'm all right, girl,' I assured her with a grin.

'You don't look all right, you look a bloody mess. You look really thin.'

'Well, I haven't been well with my sinus infection and then my tooth abscess.' I reminded Lorraine of the excuses I'd used to keep her away.

She drew in a deep breath. 'Is *he* here?' she checked. She couldn't bring herself to say his name.

'No, he's gone to community service.'

'Thank God,' she hissed. 'He always bloody butts into our conversation. Finally we have some time together.' She hugged me.

I scooped Liam into my arms as I led Lorraine into the back garden for some sunbathing. It was Thursday 21 April, the fourth hot day in a row that week, and both of us were sun worshippers, having grown up by the sea.

'Stay out of the flower beds, Liam,' I warned as I placed him down on the grass. He was now three years old and running wherever his little legs would take him. Liam played with his toys while we stretched out on the trampoline and soaked up the scorching heat.

'He's grown so much,' Lorraine said, sitting up onto her elbows.

'Yeah, too fast,' I said with a smile.

'So everything is OK with Shane?' Lorraine checked.

'Yeah, it's fine,' my voice squeaked.

'He hasn't hit you?'

'No.' I shook my head and changed the conversation. Shane would have come after me if he knew I'd opened my mouth. He might hurt my sister – I didn't know what he was capable of any more.

'Yeah, everything's great,' I lied through my teeth.

Lorraine left early afternoon, just before Shane returned in a foul mood, moaning about his community service. He switched on the telly and settled back into his favourite slouch position.

'Come out and enjoy the sun,' I said, trying to lift his mood.

'No,' he grunted.

I rolled back down on the trampoline but this time I could feel someone's eyes watching me. I looked across and Shane was glaring enviously.

'Come out,' I repeated, beckoning with my hand.

He just stared with his glacial eyes.

I tried to relax but every time I twisted my head Shane was checking up on me, watching my every move. A chill ran down my spine like someone had walked over my grave. I got up to remove myself from the line of fire and my new neighbours popped their heads over the fence.

'Hi, we haven't met properly yet,' said a lanky guy wearing board shorts and a vest.

'It's Phil and Karen,' he said, pointing to his partner who had come to join him.

'Nice to meet you,' I said nervously, knowing Shane would be watching.

'I'm Tina, and my boyfriend in there is called . . .' I said, turning around to point to the front room, but Shane was already looming behind me.

'Shane,' he said, holding his hand over the fence.

We chatted for a bit and Shane seemed to relax into his old self. He was cracking jokes and suggested that we go to the

Co-op to pick up some cans of beer. My heart leaped with happiness as I was handed a glimmer of normality again.

'I'll get Liam ready in the pushchair,' I said, beaming.

We trundled down the hilly road to the supermarket. The sun was still high and prickling our faces with its heat. We chatted about normal things; we were like a normal couple again. Our honeymoon periods had slipped from a week to just hours but I had to grab whatever I could get. We were having such a magical time that I extended our walk to take us around the back of the Co-op to the estuary.

'Let's see how far you can throw, mate,' Shane said, lifting Liam out of his pushchair.

He rummaged in the dirt for some stones and then placed one into Liam's tiny hand.

'Watch me,' Shane said, throwing a rock into the muddy estuary. He threw it so far I couldn't see it land.

'Now it's your turn, buddy.' He crouched down to help Liam. I sat on the side watching Shane play dad and my heart melted. Why can't it be like this forever? I wondered. We walked back to my place carrying the plastic bags full of booze.

'They seem all right, our new neighbours,' I chatted away.

'Yeah, he seems cool,' Shane shrugged.

We joined our new friends in the garden, them on their side of the waist-high fence, us on ours, sharing drinks and stories about the estate for hours. It was nice to see Shane laughing and not showing off for once. I left him alone for a minute while I dashed upstairs to pop my head in on Ben, who'd come back from school hours ago. He was happy watching TV in his room so I left him to it and stopped in at the upstairs loo for a wee.

The upstairs loo window overlooked the side of the house where Shane and my neighbours were nattering, so I could hear everything.

'I've got some amazing pills that help me sleep,' Shane bragged.

What the hell is he doing? I thought. I craned my ear.

'Yeah, I got Valium and sleeping tablets,' he continued, describing the pills his doctor had given him before Christmas.

Oh, for fuck's sake, I leave him for two minutes.

'Do you want to try some? I'll get you some,' he said. I heard him get up.

'No bloody way,' I said out loud. I'd just got social services off my back. I didn't need him causing problems with my neighbours. I raced down the stairs into my kitchen just at the moment Shane was reaching inside the cupboards to grab his Valium.

I snatched the bottle out of his hands, narrowed my eyes, and gave him a look to say, 'Don't you bloody dare'. He snatched them back with a punching grab.

'Oh, fuck you then,' I snapped. I threw my arms in the air out of desperation. I turned on my heels and stomped up to my bedroom. It was now 10 p.m., I was tired and fed up – I crawled under my blanket wearing my grey hooded jumper and jeans and turned on my side.

That was the last thing I remember.

I woke up horizontal across the bed with my legs hanging off the end.

What the hell?

I tried to get up but I couldn't move. I wriggled but I felt like a caterpillar stuck in a cocoon. I wriggled again but my arms were trapped by my side and something was covering my face.

What's happening? Why can't I move? Why can't I see?

The next thing I knew, two hands were clasped around my neck, strangling me. Squeezing and squeezing until my head felt like it was going to explode. Shane squeezed all the air out of me, and I passed out.

I came around gasping – I couldn't breathe, I couldn't move, I couldn't scream for help because there was no air in my lungs. My heart galloped in my ears as I was smothered by blackness. It felt like my duvet was wrapped around my body and face as tight as a sleeping bag. I wriggled like a worm on a hook but he jumped on top, pinning me down. His big hands were back around my neck, throttling me through the duvet. I was wheezing and thrashing from left to right, trying to free my hands. He tightened his grip and I passed out.

I came around for the third time and that's when I realised what was going on – Shane was killing me.

He started strangling me again and I had an out-of-body experience, as I was transported to my trampoline in the garden. I thought I could see my neighbours screaming at him to stop, as they came running to pull Shane off me. I thought I was going to be saved.

But no one came to my rescue. I passed out again.

I came around the fourth time to the sound of gargling. It was the horrible sickening sound of someone taking their last breath. I listened closely and then realised it was coming from me.

I'm dead, I'm dead.

I was so close to death my toes were curling in on themselves through spasms. I couldn't stop myself gargling. I couldn't breathe.

I don't know how I managed it, but seconds before I was about to pass out for what I'm convinced would have been the final time, I drew on some superhero strength and stretched out my right leg far enough to push off the box by my bed. I managed to lever my body up the bed and my head out of the duvet. I managed to speak a few words to save my life.

'I'm sorry, Shane, I love you,' I whispered.

He stopped in his tracks just like the times before. There was an eerie silence like the build-up in a horror film, and then he ripped the duvet off, spinning me out onto the bed. Shane spoke for the first time.

'Your eye is hanging out of your fucking head!' he shouted. 'You're blind. You're never going to see your kids again. I'm getting twenty years for this!' he yelled next to my ear.

I was in shock. I couldn't absorb his words or feel any pain. I managed to sit up and reached my hand to my face . . . and felt my eyeball hanging halfway down my cheek.

'Ugh,' I retched. None of this seemed real. I traced my fingers across to the other side of my face and my other eye was swollen to the size of a tennis ball, sticking out of my head. The entire time I was under the duvet I had no idea my eyes were gouged out.

I couldn't speak. I was in so much shock that my first reaction was to clamber to my feet and try to escape. I reached out my hands and tried to feel my way around the bed to my door.

Shane must have watched me struggle before he swooped in and grabbed my arms. Without a word, he guided me to the landing and then let me go. I dipped my toe over the edge of the stairs, like I was feeling the temperature of a pool, and then squatted down. Shane had left me to fend for myself, so I had no choice but to bum-shuffle my way down the stairs. I scraped my bum along the carpet and down a stair, scrape and then down, all the way to the bottom. Shane was there waiting for me. He yanked me up by the arm and dropped me on the sofa in the front room.

'This is all your fucking fault!' he screamed in my face. 'All this because of tablets!'

He came at me from the other side. I didn't know where he was without my eyes.

I lifted my hand up to my cheek to remind myself it wasn't just a bad dream.

'You'll never see your kids again.' His words speared my heart.

I felt my eye again, cradling it with my fingers.

Oh my God, my eye.

'It's all your fault!'

Every time he screamed at me I touched my slippery eyeball, like I couldn't believe it was real, that this was really happening to me.

'Please, Shane,' I begged, 'please let me and the kids go.' I could taste blood in my mouth but I still couldn't feel any pain.

'IT'S YOUR FUCKING FAULT!' he screamed, millimetres from my face, and I shot back into the sofa.

'Please, Shane.' I clung to my eye.

Shane ignored my pleas. I sat trembling in just my strapless bra, which was wrapped around my waist, listening to his ranting for over an hour, trying to guess where he was in the room.

'Please, Shane,' I repeated over and over again. I was begging for my life, and then I heard his feet stomp towards me like he had something planned. I cowered into the sofa but I was helpless as his brutal hands came down on me and scooped me up.

'Where are you taking me?' I whimpered, as he carried me out of the front room. He didn't say a word as he kept walking, and then he dropped me like a sack of potatoes.

SPLASH!

My head went underwater as he dumped me in my bath. I came gasping to the surface, scrabbling for the edges of the bath.

He's going to drown me, I'm dead.

The cold water went straight to my nerves and the pain shot through my body like an electric current. My eyes felt like someone had stuck a red hot poker in them. My body felt like someone had ripped out my soul. I threw up all over myself. And again, and again.

I opened my mouth to cry for help but no sound came out. I thrashed my arms around in a bath full of water and sick, fighting for my life. I managed to hook my legs over the side but I couldn't lever myself out and splashed back into the water.

Suddenly I felt Shane's big hands grip around my wrists and he yanked me out onto my feet. I wobbled in the darkness for a moment before I felt all my bodily functions go.

'Oh my God, oh my God, I'm going to go to the toilet!' I cried.

I sat over the bath and my bowels exploded.

'I'm sorry, I'm sorry, I'm sorry,' I whimpered. I was so embarrassed. It was the most degrading moment of my life.

'It's all your fault!' he shouted, as I crouched over the bath. 'All this is your fault.'

I was sick again all over myself.

19

Captive

I was so thirsty. I needed water more than I'd needed anything in my entire life. I had to stay alive for my kids. I wasn't ready to go yet.

'Please, Shane, you need to call an ambulance,' I begged. He'd brought me back into the living room after yanking me from the bath. I sat shivering on the sofa with just my bra still around my waist.

'Please, Shane, I won't tell anyone what you did. I'll say I got beaten up by two girls around the back of the Co-op.'

I was sick again all over myself.

All I could think about was getting my kids out of the house. How was I going to get them out when I couldn't see? I couldn't wake them up and scare them with my eye hanging out of my head.

'Please, Shane, I need an ambulance.'

'This is all your fucking fault,' he said again. I felt his spit on my face. 'All because of some fucking tablets.'

'Please, Shane.' I retched again. 'Please, Shane, I won't tell on you.' I wiped the vomit from my face and legs.

I felt his hot breath on my cheek as he suddenly leered up close. He stroked my cheek with his finger.

'I used to love this side of your face,' he whispered.

You sick fuck.

'You're never going to see again,' he said, continuing to stroke underneath my eyeball.

I was sick again all over myself. The pain I felt was indescribable. It was like I had the flu only magnified by a hundred times. It was as though I had a scalding poker in my empty eye socket and the bulging skin on my right eye made my face feel like it was stuck in a pressure cooker.

I was sure I was going to die.

I threw up again.

'I need water,' I whispered.

But Shane was too busy shouting blame at me. I was going to have to do it myself. If I wanted to live I had to fight. I pushed my naked body to the edge of the sofa and wobbled to my feet. Using my trembling hands, I traced my way through the living room and into the kitchen, just in time to be sick into the sink.

I felt my way into the cupboards and pulled out a pint glass and a pan from below. Every movement was as exhausting as running a marathon. I clutched the sides of the sink until I could catch my breath enough to fill up the glass with water. I downed it in one, only to be sick immediately after, but at once I felt better. It gave me enough energy to feel my way to the back door to check if it was locked.

Oh God, no.

Shane had locked it and hidden the key. There was no getting out.

I needed more water. I poured myself another pint and then carried my glass and sick pan through to the living room so I could lie down. As I shuffled along the carpet I could feel mess every-where under my feet, as if someone had ransacked my house.

'What's happened to my house?' I asked Shane, as I kicked through the debris.

No answer.

I lay my aching body on the sofa and folded my arms over my chest.

'This is your fault,' Shane started up like an engine.

My mouth was becoming a desert again.

'Why did you have to fucking open your mouth?' He was like a stuck record.

I sat up and downed the pint of water. It was soothing, like an ointment on a burn, until the deathly sick feeling rose again in my stomach. This time I was able to catch my vomit in my pan though. I pushed my deformed body onto my feet and felt my way to the kitchen to wash out the pan and fill up my glass, while listening to Shane's tirade of abuse.

I was exhausted by the time I found my way back to the sofa but I was going to die if I didn't drink water, so I forced the next pint down my throat. As soon as I was sick I stumbled to my feet and repeated the process. I must have got up and down at least fifty times through the night in between begging Shane for my life and my children's lives.

'Please, Shane, I'll tell the police I got beaten up, I promise I won't tell.'

'There's no fucking way I'm letting you out of this house,' he snapped.

Every so often I would reach my hand to my cheek and feel my eyeball slowly drying up.

It's gone, no one can save my sight now.

As every minute passed I thought I had less chance to live.

He ran that bath to drown me, to finish me off. He's not going to let me leave this house alive.

I thought about the words on his Facebook page: 'You're coming with me, dead or alive.' The memory of us watching *Hostel* the night before flashed through my mind, as did the zombie films, him punching me to the ground, him smashing my head open – round and round in my head, but I couldn't open my eyes to stop the dark images.

Shane carried on ranting and raving for what seemed like hours. It was about 4 a.m. when he finally stopped, and not long after I heard him snoring. I couldn't believe he had fallen asleep on the sofa.

I've got to get out of here. How do I get me and my kids out of here? I won't be able to get up those stairs and get my kids without waking him. I can't see my phone to call for help. I can't see, he took my eyes, I can't see.

Where the bloody hell is my hammer? It's him or me.

With every snore he grunted I wanted to pound his face and I wouldn't have stopped, I wanted him dead.

Where is it? Where did I bloody put it?

I didn't know where anything was now I had my new kitchen fitted. My hammer used to be in the cupboard by the cooker.

My blood was boiling with anger. But if I missed his face, then he would finish me off. I'd never see my kids again. My only chance was to beg him to let us go. I had to try and make it through the night without dying.

My first instinct was to build a shelter just like I used to do with my brothers and sisters when I was a kid. I patted the sofa looking for Liam's *Toy Story* blanket; I knew it was there somewhere. I tugged at the cushions and carried my armful to the corner of the room, then I propped one cushion behind my back and pulled Liam's blanket over my shivering body. It was so small it just covered me to my shins but it had the comforting smell of my little boy. I buried my nose into the soft quilt and I thought about my kids asleep upstairs. I prayed Ben hadn't heard the shouting from downstairs.

I was going to be sick again.

I don't know where I found the strength to keep pulling myself onto my feet and wash out my pan, but I did. That's how badly I wanted to live. It wasn't my time to go. As the hours crept by listening to Shane snore I kept feeling my face, thinking about his words: 'You'll never see your kids again.' I wiped my nose and felt something stringy stick to my fingers. I thought it must be snot so I tried to pull it away but the string just kept coming out of my nose.

Oh my God, it's my optical nerves, I realised, holding a handful of stringy veins.

I was sick all over myself.

Oh God, please help me.

I'd lost count of the number of times I'd been sick by the time Shane woke up. The birds were tweeting so I knew it must have been around 7 a.m. I'd been blind and held captive for eight hours.

'Oh my God, look at the state of your face,' Shane said, with his croaky just-woken-up voice.

'You're blind,' he said.

He got up and knelt down beside me. He smelled disgusting.

'I used to love this side of your face,' he repeated, seeming obsessed with it. He stroked underneath my eyeball again.

My upper lip curled with disgust.

'Please, Shane, please can you call an ambulance,' I started begging again.

He took a deep breath and spoke very calmly.

'You're not allowed to call an ambulance but I'll let you call Paul and he can take you to hospital,' he decided.

It didn't make sense, but I wasn't about to argue my lifeline away.

'Thank you, Shane, thank you. I promise I won't tell the police anything.'

'This was all your fault,' he reminded me.

'I know,' I said, going along with it, 'I'm sorry.' I just had to get out alive.

'My mobile is in my bag,' I told him.

'I have your phone here,' he said. I could hear him playing with something in his hands.

'Please, Shane, can you ring Paul?' I begged.

He didn't say anything but kept playing with my phone like he was teasing me.

'Please, Shane.'

'All because of those fucking tablets,' he finally spoke. He was back to ranting and raving.

My heart sank as I felt like a ship drifting out to sea. I had him, I nearly had him. I didn't have any energy left to start all over again.

'Please, Shane, please.' I tried to change the tone of my voice to sound calmer.

'What?' he was angry again. 'There's no credit on your phone.'

'Use my bank card, please, I'll do anything for you,' I gasped.

I heard him rummaging in what must have been my handbag. Shane asked for my bank details but for some reason wasn't adding the credit. He was dangling a carrot in front of my nose, the sick fuck. I begged for ages until I heard the sound of someone stirring.

Oh God, Ben's waking up for school. He can't see me like this, help.

'Shane, you have to take me back upstairs. I can't let the kids see me like this,' I pleaded.

He blew out an irritated sigh, but I knew he loved my kids, not even he would wish that on them. He grabbed my arm and yanked me from my den. I clung on to Liam's blanket like it was the most precious thing in the world while he led me up to my bedroom. I gently lowered myself onto the mattress while Shane left me to go and speak to Ben.

'Have you got any credit on your phone?' he asked my boy. I didn't know why he didn't just put it on my mobile hours ago, but I was relieved he was finally helping me.

'No.' I could tell Ben was frightened.

'Can you run down to your Nan's and ring up Paul, and get him to ring *your* phone, not your mum's,' he demanded.

'Oh, OK,' Ben stammered.

'Don't you dare say anything to your Nan that something is going on,' he snapped.

'What?' Ben didn't know what he was talking about, thank God.

'Don't say anything,' he barked.

The house fell into silence for those ten minutes Ben was at Nan's. Shane must have been downstairs waiting for him, as I couldn't hear his breathing. My breathing was shallow and rasping like I was on the edge of death.

'Come on, Ben, come on, boy.' He was my last chance.

I heard a knock on the door as Shane let Ben back inside and then Shane ran up the stairs and pressed Ben's mobile into my hand. Two seconds later it sang.

'All right?' Paul's voice was music to my ears.

'No, can you take me to the hospital please,' I whispered with my last breaths.

'Yep, I'll be there in a minute,' he said. He knew something was very wrong.

As I lay there listening to my heartbeat, I could hear Shane running up and down the stairs collecting his belongings.

'Where the fuck is it?' he shouted, pulling things off the shelves.

I pulled Liam's little quilt up to my neck as I waited for Paul to save me. He must have driven like lightning from Penzance, as he was knocking at my door ten minutes later.

'Fuck,' I heard Shane spit.

I craned my ear to hear Paul insert the front-door key I didn't know he had. My heart raced as I saw the finishing line.

'Where is she?' Paul snarled.

He didn't wait for an answer and bounded up the stairs as Shane trailed after him, whimpering pathetically.

'Two girls beat her up behind the Co-op,' said Shane limply.

Paul stormed into the boys' room and scooped Liam into his arms.

Oh God, please don't bring Liam in here.

It was too late.

'Oh my God!' Paul shouted.

I turned my head to hide my face from Liam and felt my eye fall onto the bed. Liam started screaming.

'I'm ringing an ambulance, I'm going to get help!' Paul shouted as he ran down the stairs with Liam in his arms.

I was gasping for water again. I shimmied myself to the edge of the bed, and this time I could feel Shane staring at me. I knew he was watching me; I just didn't know where he was. I reached both my hands out in front of me as I shuffled to the door. I could smell him, I was getting close, and then my fingers touched something hard – his chest – as he guarded my door.

He smelled of fear. There was no way he would finish me off with Paul in the house. I pushed forward and he backed off like the coward he really was. I bum-shuffled my way down the stairs again. The whole time Shane was in front of me, promising to be there for me.

'I'll meet you at the hospital,' he said over and over, before running out of my front door.

I could hear Paul talking to the boys in the front yard as I collapsed on my sofa. My boys are safe, I thought, my boys are safe, and I relaxed. I felt myself floating above my body, floating into another world. I wondered if this was finally The End.

'Arrrrrrghh!' My neighbour Zara's piercing scream brought me down to earth.

I heard footsteps running back out of my house and then more feet. I must have looked like something out of a horror film, lying there naked with my eye hanging out.

'Water, I need water,' I begged.

'Don't worry, Tina, an ambulance is on its way.' It was Zara's unmistakable Northern accent. I could feel her by my side and then she stroked my arm.

'Hang in there,' she said. Her voice was warm and loving and would have made me cry if only I could. She then reached her arms underneath my waist and unclipped my strapless bra.

'This is a bit pointless, Tina,' she joked, pulling it away. Zara must have pulled some clothes out of my cupboard as she then tried to dress me, giving me some of my dignity back.

'Thanks, Zara,' I whispered.

I heard the ambulance siren in the background. I was safe. I could finally relax after twelve hours of being held hostage.

I was lifted onto a stretcher as what sounded like hundreds of people ran around me. Cops, paramedics, neighbours . . . it sounded like chaos. I heard my name, I heard Shane's name – my head was spinning.

'Breathe this,' a man said, putting a mask over my face. I gulped the oxygen like it was water and the noise faded away into nothingness.

20

Hospital

I came round to the noise of machines bleeping, feet rushing around my bed, people talking over me, about me, things being stuck in my arm. I was awake but it was like I was on a different planet.

'Water, I want water,' I mumbled through my morphine haze.

Police forensics surrounded me, taking swabs from my mouth and under my fingernails.

'Tina, can you tell us what happened to you?' a man with a gruff voice demanded.

'I want water,' I said again.

'Tina, it's the police. We need to know where Shane Jenkin is,' he went on.

Just the mention of his name sent me into blind panic. I couldn't let the cops know what had really happened or Shane would kill me. My heart raced with fear.

'Two girls beat me up around the back of the Co-op,' I recited.

More people prodded my skin. I felt wet bandages cover my eyes. I was sick again. I couldn't stop throwing up, my insides felt on fire.

'Tina, we need you to tell us the truth so we can catch Shane,' the cop badgered.

'Water, water,' I begged. 'I just got roughed up underneath the duvet, that's all.' I rolled my head from side to side.

'GIVE ME SOME FUCKING WATER!' I screamed, rising off the bed.

'Please,' I pleaded. In my mind, I was sure that water was the only thing that was going to keep me alive. I had no choice. I was forced to tell the truth.

'Shane did this to me,' I finally whimpered.

'Where is he, Tina?' the gruff cop demanded.

'I don't know, I don't know.' I shook my head.

I felt a damp sponge on my lips and I sucked on it like an ice lolly. The cool water soothed my arid mouth. Shane was going to kill me.

Suddenly feet were running everywhere and people were shouting.

'No, Shane, no, Shane,' a nurse cried.

Oh God, he's come to finish me off.

I screamed as I wrapped my arms over my face.

'No, Tina, it's OK, it's not him.' Hands were pulling my arms down.

The nurse explained that a patient who also happened to be called Shane was on the same ward, and having an epileptic fit. I couldn't stop shaking, I thought Shane had heard me tell the police and had come to kill me. I must have been injected with more drugs, as the next thing I remember is the sound of my family crying around my bed.

'Oh, Tine.' Lorraine's hand was shaking as she stroked my foot.

'That fucking monster,' my mum cried.

'Water, please can you give me water?' I begged my family.

'This is all my fault. I should have known something was wrong when I saw you yesterday,' Lorraine sobbed.

'Water . . .' I was absorbing their distress and it was making me feel even sicker.

'Why aren't they operating on her to save her eyes?' Mum screamed.

I vomited over myself.

I knew my left eye was gone. I'd felt it dry up over the twelve hours Shane had kept me hostage. It was still hanging out of my head, covered with a bandage. I was certain my right eye was going to be OK though, that it was just swollen from him punching me in the face.

I had no idea Shane had gouged both my eyes out. I thought he'd throttled me so hard one eye had popped out. I'm going to be OK, I thought, I'm going to see my kids again.

More hours passed in a haze. Tracey arrived at 6 p.m. and ran out of the cubicle as soon as she saw my mangled face. I'd been told my nose was smashed, and the doctors weren't sure they would be able to save my eyelid, let alone my dangling eye.

It was Mum who eventually broke the news that she had been asked to sign the operating consent form.

'They want to remove your left eye,' she said, choking back the tears.

A deathly sick feeling rose into my mouth. I knew my eye was buggered but hearing I was going to lose it was too much to bear. I couldn't cry though, my eyes wouldn't let me, I just howled with misery. Lorraine and Tracey started crying again as they heard my pain.

'It's going to be OK,' Tracey promised.

'Put me to sleep, I've had enough.' I begged my sisters to kill me.

'No, Tina, we love you,' Lorraine cried.

'Put me to sleep,' I said over and over, as the nurse sedated me.

My eye had been hanging out of my head for over twenty hours by the time they eventually operated at 7.40 p.m. There was nothing left except a dry shrivelled ball. I clung on to the hope that at least I still had my right eye.

I came round from my anaesthetic to the sound of my sisters calling my name. It was like I was standing at the end of a long dark tunnel and their echo took forever to reach me. I wanted to open my eyes and wake up, but then I remembered I had no eyes to open and I was stuck in the darkness. It was the lowest I had felt since Shane attacked me. I wanted to cry but I couldn't; all I could do was make the noises that should have gone with my tears.

'It's OK, Tina, we're here,' Tracey said. But her voice was nervous and shaky, making me even more upset. 'The operation went well,' she continued, and tried to calm me by stroking my hand.

I didn't care if they'd cut my eye off successfully, I just wanted it back. I wanted to take everything back. I knew I was playing with fire with Shane but I never thought I'd get burned this badly. Why? Why did he do this to me?

'The doctor said he managed to save your eyelid,' Lorraine said.

'Oh, great, I have an eyelid but no eye,' I whimpered.

From across the room I heard my name being called by what sounded like a rasping old lady.

'Tina, Tina,' she cried out.

I was so disorientated from the drugs, the pain, the feeling of loss.

'Don't worry, Tina, you can get a glass eye like me,' she said.

Her words were like a spear through my heart. I know she only meant well but it was the last thing I needed to hear. I just thought, shut up. At least I still had my right eye though; at least I'd still be able to see Liam and Ben again.

My family stayed by my bedside all night as I faded in and out of consciousness. When I wasn't sleeping I was begging for water or throwing up. I was too ill to think much more about Shane – I just had to survive the night.

I woke up with that familiar sick feeling I'd had almost every day for the past year, where you remember everything from the night before, only this time I couldn't open my eyes to escape the nightmare. I had Lorraine by my bed to hold me down as I vomited in distress.

I was relieved when the doctor came in to check on me. I needed him to tell me I was going to be OK, that I was going to see again.

'We managed to save your eyelid,' he said softly. I clutched Lorraine's hand as I listened.

'But I'm afraid we think your tear ducts are damaged beyond repair,' he said.

'So she'll never be able to cry again?' Lorraine yelped.

'No.'

'But what about my right eye, doctor?' I whispered.

'There is a lot of blood covering it at the moment, so when that submerges we'll have a better idea,' he said matter-of-factly. 'We know he didn't manage to gouge it out but we just don't know what condition it's in.'

What? He tried to gouge my eyes out? Up until that moment I still had no idea what had happened to me. I thought my right eye was just badly swollen from Shane's punches.

The surgeon drew in a deep breath and told me he'd never seen a case like it. 'He would have had to use extreme force to do this,' he said. I remembered what the doctor had told me almost a year ago to the day – that it was virtually impossible to gouge someone's eyes out while they were awake.

'I'll be able to see again, won't I?' I begged.

He took another long pause. 'We just don't know at the moment, Tina.'

My heart felt crushed. I couldn't cope with hearing that, so I blocked out his words and kept on believing it was going to be OK.

'I'm going to see again, Lorraine, I know I am . . .' My voice petered out.

By the end of the second day in hospital, the news of what Shane had done to me had spread like wildfire. I had two cops with Taser guns guarding my room from Shane and from journalists who were trying to snap pictures of me on my deathbed. The nurses told me how reporters had tried to sneak onto my ward by pretending to be work-experience students.

'I don't want anyone seeing me like this,' I wailed.

'Don't worry, Tine, no one is going to hurt you,' Lorraine promised.

But I was still petrified that Shane *was* going to hurt me. He'd been on the run for two days now and had promised he would come to the hospital, those were his last words to me.

'The dead can't speak,' I mumbled.

'What are you on about, Tine?' asked Lorraine.

'If he finishes me off then it won't be my word against his. He wants me dead.'

Both my sisters touched me to calm me down. Tracey stroked my arm and said there was nothing to worry about – I had two big, burly policemen guarding my door.

'He can't get you, you're safe,' Tracey reassured me.

'Tracey's right,' came a voice I recognised from across the room. It was Lara Pimm from the domestic violence unit. She pulled up a chair beside my bed, and although I couldn't see her I could feel her caring warmth.

'We've got police looking everywhere. Anyone who knows him is being questioned,' she said. I could smell her shampoo as she leaned forward.

'We think Shane tried to cover up the attack by staging a burglary in your house,' Lara revealed.

'What do you mean?' I said, sitting up urgently.

Lara explained how Shane had turned my house upside down so he could hide the evidence of the attack. He turned over my mattress and hid my bloody bed sheets in the shed at the bottom of my garden. Lara revealed that he had used such force gouging out my eyes that he had broken the wooden slats under my mattress.

'So he pushed me through my bed?' I asked. The thought made me retch again. 'The sick bastard, I can't believe he's done this to me. Why has he done this?'

'We're going to get him, Tina,' she said, and cupped my hand.

I had no real idea of night and day because there were family and friends by my side around the clock. My boys were staying with Paul and I banned them from seeing me until I was a bit better. Everyone else who came to visit me shook like a leaf when they sat by my side. I needed to call on my inner fighter and be strong for them.

'Is it cold outside?' I teased my best friend Danni as I felt her hands shake.

'I can't get anything past you, Tina,' Danni sniffed. 'I can't believe he did this to you. It's my fault, I should have done more to try and get him out of your life.' She broke down.

Everyone was blaming themselves but I was the only one to blame.

'I made my bed, I've got to lie in it now,' I said, trying to be strong. 'I wasn't listening to anyone.' I took a sip of my icy juice; it was the only thing I could hold down. I'd been told my tongue was black from biting down on it so hard while Shane was throttling me.

'You not eating?' Danni sounded worried.

'No, I'm on a diet,' I joked, and I heard her snigger through her sniffles.

I could be strong while everyone was around me because they stopped me thinking about the reality of my situation. They helped me not think about Shane and where he was, what he was doing. They helped me feel protected while the police carried out their manhunt.

Shane was finally the outlaw he had always dreamed of being. I was constantly asking the cops on my door for updates and they revealed how they had missed Shane by minutes. Apparently he was jumping between safe houses like lily pads.

I had been in hospital for four days when the police shouted out to me that they'd 'got him'.

'Where? Where is he?' I asked, sitting up. It was the most alert I'd felt for days. I heard the crackle of the walkie-talkies as the information was relayed.

'What are they saying? Lorraine, what are they saying?' I demanded. The suspense was killing me.

'They've found him in a house in Trenear,' the officer on my door informed me.

'Is he hurt?' I asked. After months of abuse it was ingrained in me to ask about his well-being.

'I hope they fucking kill him,' Mum shouted.

'We don't know at the moment,' said the policeman. 'The house is surrounded with armed police.'

It was just like Raoul Moat. Shane was going to get what he wished for – he was going to go out in a blaze of glory. I despised him but I didn't wish him dead, my heart wasn't ready for that.

'Are they going to shoot him?' I shrieked.

'I hope they take out his eyes,' Mum said, pacing the room.

'He isn't believed to be armed,' the officer said through the walkie-talkie crackle.

I was on tenterhooks as the information was slowly drip-fed to me. My room filled up with friends and family as the news snowballed around town. My sisters were holding my hands when the police finally revealed Shane Jenkin had been arrested.

The first thing I felt was relief that he wasn't going to finish me off. And then sadness washed over me as I thought about what a waste it had all been. I was blind and he was going to be banged up for a long time. I'd put up with his beatings for nothing. Shane promised me he'd change, that we would live happily ever after, but he'd lied. It had all been lies.

My hospital room had turned into a circus with friends and police coming and going. The noises were exhausting, and hearing Shane's name over and over again was distressing – I just wanted to be alone to grieve. Just when I thought I'd heard all there was to know, a family friend came bursting into my room with more news of the arrest. Dan had actually seen Shane being carted off to the nick.

'You should have seen his face, Tina,' he said, still breathless.

I was going to be sick again.

'The police had him surrounded for forty minutes so word got out and everyone dropped what they were doing and drove to Trenear to see him pay for what he did to you. There were a couple of hundred people waiting outside that house for him,' he shrieked.

Half a dozen people let out gasps. I hugged my sick bowl ready for my explosion.

'When he finally came out he had this big smirk on his face like he thought he was a hero,' he continued.

'And then everyone turned on him.'

'What do you mean?' I said, choking on my words.

'Everyone started hurling abuse at him, calling him a fucking bastard. I wish you could have been there, Tina, his face just dropped. He put his head down like a coward and the police had to guard him as they led him to the van. Everyone wanted him dead.'

I couldn't believe how hated he was. I'd been in a bubble in hospital, I didn't think anyone would have cared that much about what he'd done to me.

'They were rocking the police van as he was taken away. All hell broke loose,' Dan said.

So he didn't go out in a blaze of glory after all. He shrank into the coward he really was.

'He would have hated being humiliated like that,' I said, and smiled at my small victory.

21

Buried Alive

It was the moment of truth – I was going to find out if I would ever see again.

As the doctor unwrapped the bandage from around my eyes my heart was beating in my mouth I was so nervous. He gently lifted my swollen face and rested my chin on a machine that felt like a telescope. I touched my eye and it was still as big as a tennis ball. I must have looked like a freaky insect with my bulge. I must have looked hideous.

'I'm going to shine the light into your eye and you have to tell me if you see anything,' the doctor explained.

I couldn't bear the waiting any longer, I just needed him to get on with it – I needed to know if I would see again.

Please God, please God, please God, I prayed.

I heard switches being flicked and buttons being pressed and then the doctor adjusted my chin slightly.

'Don't be afraid,' he said gently. 'OK, ready?'

'Ready as I'll ever be,' I joked.

I heard some clicks and waited for the light. But the light was already shining in my eye.

'Can you see it?' he asked.

'No,' I replied.

There were some more noises. 'How about that?' he asked again.

'No.' My voice was crumbling.

There was a pause as he changed some more settings on the telescope.

'How about now?' he tried again.

'No,' I said, trembling with disappointment.

'OK, that's enough for now,' he said, gently pulling my chin away. I dropped my head like a puppet whose strings had broken.

'I'm never going to see again, am I, doctor?' I whimpered.

'There's still a lot of blood there, that might be masking your vision,' he told me. He tried to sound hopeful.

It wasn't much but it was the crumb of hope I needed to carry on. My sisters and Mum were anxiously waiting for me on my ward and I felt the pressure to be strong for them. They crowded around my bed, doing their best to stifle their tears.

'At least I'll never see myself get old, I'll be thirty-one forever,' I joked.

They tried to laugh along with me.

'And none of you will age either, you'll stay young and beautiful in my eyes,' I smiled.

Lorraine broke down sobbing.

'It's still me, I'm still here,' I said, forcing myself to be strong. 'And all isn't lost yet, they're doing a scan tomorrow to see what condition my eye is in.'

But the scan the following day was more heartbreaking. The doctor performed what he likened to an ultrasound on a pregnant woman, on my eyeball.

'It's not the right shape,' he sighed as he moved the equipment across my swollen eye. 'It's been squashed out of shape.' He carried on checking.

I knew in my heart I was never going to see again – Shane had pressed his thumbs so hard into my eyes he'd squished my right eyeball into my head. But I wasn't ready to face the truth yet; I couldn't deal with the idea of never seeing my boys again. What mother could? I plunged into denial, and hoped a solution would be found. I took the fact that the doctors wouldn't be removing my squashed eyeball as a sign of hope. I told myself when the swelling and the blood went down I'd be able to see again.

'I know I'm going to see again,' I told my family. 'Shane will not be the last person I ever see,' I said defiantly.

Whether they believed it or not they all went along with it to give me strength. I couldn't have gone on if it hadn't been for my family supporting me every second of the way. My sisters held my hands when Lara dropped by to tell me Shane had been charged with GBH with intent. He was locked up in Exeter Prison until his plea hearing in July.

'There is no way in hell he will plead guilty,' I snapped. 'He thinks he's invincible.

'He's going to bloody hate it being on the wing with all the wrong 'uns, with the paedophiles and the rapists. He's spent enough time in prison, he knows what it's all about, and he knows being on that wing means he's a sicko too.' It was another small victory I could enjoy while I lay helpless in my hospital bed.

'Let him rot in hell,' Lorraine hissed.

But it was me who was rotting in hell. Having your sight snatched away from you is like a living hell. Every day I woke up in hospital hoping this would be the day that I'd see the light from the doctor's telescope. But every day my dreams were shattered as all I could see was eternal darkness. And by the evening I wanted to tear my hair out because the blackness had become too much to bear. I couldn't close my eyelids to rest; often I didn't know whether I was awake or sleeping.

I felt like I'd been buried alive.

It helped having a twenty-four-hour vigil around my bed because I always had someone to talk to, to touch for comfort, to stop me sinking into depression, to stop me thinking about Shane. I hadn't been alone since arriving at the hospital, so I didn't know what to expect when there would be no one to reach out to.

Paul had been looking after me that night but he needed to go home to tuck my boys into bed. I still didn't want them seeing me, as I'd been told my head looked like a lollipop on a stick.

'You sure you'll be fine?' he checked one last time.

'Yeah, kiss Ben and Liam goodnight for me,' I said, shooing him away. I'd been in hospital for a couple of weeks and I was sure I could get through a night by myself. How bad could it be?

I had so many drugs pumping around my body that my face, arms and legs felt numb and floppy. But my mind was still switched on and my ears were pricked now hearing had taken over as my primary sense. I lay there listening to my hospital ward shut down for the night, wishing I could switch my whirring thoughts off too. The voices of visiting families were the first to go and pretty soon I didn't even have the nurses' squeaking shoes along the hall for comfort. All I had was the noise of a pumping ventilator keeping someone alive.

'I'm so buggered,' I whimpered. It was the first chance I'd had to think about what it would be like to be blind and I wanted to die.

I'll never be able to walk again, go to the toilet, wash myself without help.

I'd never been around someone who was blind so I had no clue how someone can cope with this eternal darkness. I thought about Ben and Liam's little faces and how I was going to have them taken away from me. If I didn't have my kids, then what was the point in living?

I rolled my head from side to side on the pillow trying to shake off my painful thoughts but I'd opened the floodgates. I imagined Shane's snarling face looming in like he was in the hospital room with me.

'You bastard,' I said, wishing I could cry tears.

Why? Why had he done this to me? Every time he'd attacked me in the past Shane had made me feel like I was to blame, but I knew this time it wasn't my fault. I'd gone up to bed and he came looking for me once I was asleep. My heart thumped as I ran through the events of that night. It was a premeditated silent attack, it wasn't my fault – I didn't deserve this.

'Oh my God,' I breathed, breaking the deathly silence of the hospital.

A light bulb had gone on in my head as I finally pieced together what Shane had done to me. He'd gouged my eyes out before he wrapped me in the duvet, I realised, shaking my head in disbelief.

I'd gone to bed and then Shane came upstairs, jumped on top of me while I was sleeping, punched me around the face until I was unconscious and then gouged my eyes out with his thumbs. He then wrapped me up in the duvet because he thought I was dead. He didn't expect me to wake up, so when I did he had to finish me off. The duvet saved my life in the end because it stopped him getting a killer grip around my throat.

'And then he ran that bath to drown me,' I gasped.

I grabbed my sick pan as I felt the vomit rush out of me.

I bet Shane wishes I was dead now, I thought. He'll be in his prison cell kicking himself that he didn't kill me that night.

'Well, I survived, you bastard, I'm still alive and kicking,' I snapped.

'Is everything OK, Tina?' a nurse said; she must have popped her head around the door.

'Yeah,' I lied. I just wanted my sisters, I couldn't bear being alone with my thoughts. I spent the whole night thinking about Shane and performing an autopsy on the events of that night. I had no idea when I finally drifted off to sleep but I was woken by the thunderous sound of a helicopter hovering overhead.

The whirring noise of the chopper blades jolted me awake and for a split second I thought I could see the cream ceiling, the door of my hospital room, the window and the orange lights from the helicopter shining through the blinds.

'I can see,' I cried, reaching out my arms.

And then it vanished into blackness.

'I can see, I can see,' I said over and over again.

'Tina, are you OK in there?' It was the nurse checking on me again.

'I can see, I saw my hospital room,' I gasped, breathless with excitement.

'What did you see?' she asked, tucking my sheet back in.

'I saw the ceiling and the door and the window,' I told her, beaming.

'That's brilliant, Tina, now just rest and the doctor will examine you later.' She filled up my glass with icy water and left.

Rest? How can I rest?

I needed to tell everyone that I was going to be OK. It seemed like hours before the doctor put me under his special telescope.

'No,' I said, as he shone the light.

'No,' I repeated, as he shone another beam.

The wheels on his chair screeched as he pushed away from the machine.

'I saw my hospital room, doctor, how can you explain that?' I begged.

The doctor sighed heavily and explained how sometimes the mind plays tricks, and when the body is fighting so hard to see, you can imagine what things would look like.

His words were like a pin in a balloon. My heart went pop and I shrank back into my wheelchair.

I cleared my throat and poured out my heart: 'Whether it was real or not, I'm thankful, because it means Shane wasn't the last thing I saw.'

22

Life on the Other Side

'Over my dead body are they taking my kids away from me,' I shouted.

The lady from social services tried to calm me down.

'No one is going to take your children away from you, Tina. That would be discrimination, there are plenty of blind people out there raising children,' she said.

She sounded much friendlier than the woman who had turned up on my doorstep last year.

'So no one is going to take them away?' I checked, trembling with relief.

'No one is taking your children from you. We'll have to appoint a carer to help, but we'll discuss that further when you move into your new house.' I could hear her smile through her words.

Thanks to Lara from the domestic violence unit fighting my corner, the council had allocated me a new place to live so I wouldn't have to face going back to that house of horrors. The three-bed house was on an estate outside Penzance, and the best bit was I knew what it was like inside because I'd had a look around it when I first moved back to the neighbourhood. The bad news was I had to wait four months until I could move in.

'So you'll be going to this rehabilitation hospital in . . .' the social services lady took a moment to flick through her notes, '. . . in Redruth.'

'No way,' I said defiantly. 'Now I know my kids will be safe I'm not staying a minute longer away from them.'

I told the lady I would be discharging myself at the end of my third week and I'd take turns living with my sister Lorraine and best friend Danielle until I moved into my new house. I wasn't going to have my kids put into care while I sat rotting in a hospital bed. No way, I was going to make up to them for all the harm I'd caused.

'Tina, I know you want to be with your children but what you're proposing could be very disorientating and distressing for you,' she said, sounding concerned.

'I'm not lying in hospital a minute longer than I have to,' I said. The fighter was coming again. There was no arguing with me when I got an idea in my head. When someone told me I couldn't do something I'd go out of my way to prove them wrong.

It was time I was reunited with my boys. I asked Paul if he could bring Ben and Liam into the hospital after school that day. I'd missed them so much I couldn't wait to hug them and reassure them everything would be OK. I kept asking my sisters how bad I looked in the run-up to them arriving at the hospital because I didn't want my boys to be scared of their mummy.

'Do I look like a monster?' I asked, touching my swollen face.

'I won't lie to you, Tine, you have looked better,' Lorraine joked.

'You're still you, Tine, you're their mum and they love you,' Tracey chipped in.

It was one of those moments when I wished I could cry.

Paul popped his head round the door and said the boys were waiting outside.

'Ben is really upset,' he said, and paused. 'He wants you to put your sunglasses on.'

'Oh, OK,' I mumbled, feeling for my glasses with the diamante stars. I slipped them on and propped another pillow behind my back.

'OK, I'm ready,' I said nervously.

I heard the patter of little feet running into the room and Liam's happy voice.

'Mummy!' he screamed with joy.

'Hi, Liam,' I said, giving him a big smile and stretching out my hand into nothingness.

I wanted my eyes back so badly. It was torture hearing my boy's voice but not being able to see him. I had to imagine what he looked like and my memory was already fading from the trauma of the attack. Paul lifted him onto my bed and he wrapped his little arms around my neck.

'Careful, Liam,' Paul said, but the pain was worth every second of Liam's warm body. I loved how he didn't care that his mummy looked like a freak.

'Ben?' I called out.

I heard a sniffle as Ben tried to stifle his sobs by the door.

'It's all right, Ben, I'm still here,' I said, and beckoned him over.

Ben was crying and shaking as he sat next to my bed. Hearing my boy in distress but not being able to see his sad face was almost too much to bear. I bit my lip to stop it trembling.

'I'm going to be OK,' I reassured him.

'I love you, Mum,' he sobbed.

A couple of days later I discharged myself from Truro Hospital and moved into Lorraine's place with her ten-year-old son Bradley and Nathan, who was six. I was determined to prove the social worker wrong, that I could manage without twenty-four-hour care and my own house. The kids would sleep at Paul's and spend the days with me.

'Don't make a fuss over me,' I told my family. 'Just tell me if I'm in your way. I don't want to be a burden on anyone,' I insisted, pleading for them to get on with their own lives.

I started out strong, thinking I could take on the world, but I quickly realised that I was going to need their support just to get through the basics of life. I could go to the loo by myself and the nurses had taught me how to wash my body and face, but I needed my sister to dress me and tell me when I was putting something on back to front or inside out. It was so frustrating not having a clue where anything was in Lorraine's house. It's incredible how little you absorb when you take your memory for granted. I bet if you close your eyes now you wouldn't be able to list five objects in your best friend's living room.

I counted my steps from the kitchen to the living room but I still kept bashing my shoulder into the door frame and my knees into the sofa arm. It was easier to sit in the same spot all day long and I built my nest on a chair in Lorraine's kitchen.

'Have some soup,' Lorraine said, pushing a bowl of creamed tomato under my nose. Just the smell made me want to vomit again.

'I'm not hungry,' I said, pushing it away with my fingers.

'You've got to eat,' she insisted.

'I can't eat, I can't stop throwing my guts up,' I snapped. I felt like such a cripple.

The only thing I wanted was tea. I'd drink cup after cup all day long while staring into the nothingness that my life had become. The worst part of it all was I couldn't play with Liam when he called out for me. I couldn't help Ben with his homework, make dinner for them, see whether my boys were smiling or sad – I couldn't be there for my kids like I used to be, and it was eating me up from the inside.

I had a constant stream of visitors who would distract my bleak thoughts with stories of what was going on in their lives, what the latest gossip was. I used to have a short attention span but now I could sit and listen for hours. I was living through others to get me through my day.

I'd repeatedly lift my hand up to my face, hoping I could see it, while people would be chatting to me. I kept thinking I could see shadows and would stand in the same spot for a while, praying they would return. But they never did. The worst time was at night though, that's when my dreams would tease me. I'd wake up shouting that I could see, with my arms stretched out in front of me. Lorraine would come running in because she thought I was crying out in pain.

'I can see, I can see,' I yelled after I dreamed I was looking at the sea from her bedroom window.

'It's OK, Tina,' Lorraine said, cradling my head.

'But I saw the blue,' I pleaded.

She stroked my hair and my heart sank as I realised it was yet another dream. I got the lump in my throat that usually came when I was about to cry and then a hot burning sensation bled into where my eyes should have been.

'No, no, no, don't let me cry!' I screamed in pain.

I dug my nails into the bed covers as I squirmed in agony. It felt like pouring salt into an open wound.

'I'm not supposed to be able to cry,' I squealed.

'Calm down, Tina,' Lorraine ordered, trying to bring me back to earth.

I buried my head into my pillow until the feeling passed. Lorraine lay next to me, stroking my back until I eventually fell asleep. My safe hospital bubble had burst and I was now falling into a place much darker than the world I was living in.

I started thinking I would have been better off dead. That Shane should have finished me off that night. That I was a burden on all those around me. Danielle and my sister did their best to make me feel at home when I was with them but I felt guilty for troubling them even for a cup of tea. I was too proud to ask Lorraine for help when I got lost in her house.

'Ouch,' I said as I banged into something hard.

This isn't Lorraine's bedroom, I thought. I'd gone upstairs one evening to take a phone call with Lara and I didn't know where I was. I reached out my hands like a zombie and felt a wooden frame as high as my head. I scratched my hands in the air like a dog paddling, trying to feel what it was. I felt something soft, something move . . .

Oh my God, I'm in the kids' bedroom.

I'd bumped into the bunk bed and I didn't know how to get out. I turned around, shuffled forward and stubbed my toe. I bit my arm to stop myself screaming and waking Nathan. I turned around again, shuffled forward and hit my nose on something sharp. My heart started to race as that familiar trapped feeling returned.

It was like being back under the duvet. Being locked in my panic room. Being trapped under Shane's twenty-stone body. *Help, help, help,* I cried silently. I moved forward again but this time my fingers snapped onto what felt like a door handle.

'Yes,' I whispered as relief washed over me. I pulled the door open and stepped through . . . into a faceful of coat hangers. I was now in the kids' wardrobe. The hot burning feeling rose in my eyes again as I didn't want to cry for help but didn't know how to escape. I dropped to the floor and crawled on my hands and knees to where I hoped the door would be. God took pity on me and finally showed me the way out. Exhausted, I rolled over onto my back in the hallway as the tears burned the holes in my eyes.

I turned to sleeping tablets to get me through the lonely nights and higher doses of painkillers to ease me through the day. But no drug could numb the pain I felt in my heart for Shane. As his plea hearing approached, not a second of the day would pass without me thinking about him. His twisted face was the last thing I saw before I went to sleep, and his puppy-dog eyes were the first thing I saw when I woke up in the morning. I hated him but, like a drug addict being weaned off heroin, I still needed him. I wanted him to ring me from prison and tell me how sorry he was and beg me to forgive him. The worst part was, I had to keep my feelings locked up inside my dark world because I was too ashamed to admit I hadn't let go yet.

It had been two and a half months since the attack, since I'd heard Shane's final words, 'I'll see you at the hospital.' I didn't know if I was strong enough to be in the same courtroom as him but the warrior in me wanted to be there to show him I wasn't backing down this time. It was the only way I could think of to get the ghost of Shane out of my system.

'You don't have to do this,' Lara reminded me again as I sat in the witness protection room of Truro Crown Court. 'It's just the plea hearing,' she explained.

'I know,' I said. 'But I want Shane to know I'm not backing down this time. He's not getting away with it again.'

Lara squeezed my trembling hand. My mind was thinking one thing, but my body was saying another – that I was terrified.

'Shane's arrived,' announced one of the cops in the room. My heart started galloping as the adrenalin kicked in.

'Does he know I'm here?' I asked tentatively.

'He's just been told,' said the cop. He sounded in his late thirties and slightly overweight. I'd started to imagine how people looked according to their voice.

'And he ain't happy about it,' he went on.

'Oh right,' I said. I shook as I imagined Shane's face screwing up like when he was just about to hit me.

'He's kicked off down in the cells, sacked his legal team,' the cop scoffed.

'He's trying to intimidate me, scare me into keeping my mouth shut,' I said, turning to Lara. 'I know that's what he's doing.' I'd seen it so many times before.

'He can sack his legal team for all I care, I'm not backing down,' I said, and straightened my back.

Lara and Anna Onslow from the domestic violence team lifted me by my arms and guided me into the courtroom. I shuffled at a snail's pace up the stairs and into the public gallery where my family were sitting in the back row. The room fell silent as I could feel everyone's eyes watching me struggle.

'You're nearly there,' Lara whispered in my ear.

'Everyone's watching me,' I whimpered.

'Keep going,' she urged. Lara kept me strong.

I slid along the bench and waited for Shane to appear. I thought I could hear a clock ticking. There was some coughing from my right and a man in the front row cleared his throat. Lara squeezed my arm as I heard footsteps.

Oh God, it must be Shane.

I heard the sound of pens scribbling furiously on paper. Lara had said there might be reporters from the papers there.

'Are you Shane Jenkin?' the judge asked.

My heart was in my mouth as I waited for him to speak.

'Yeah,' he muttered.

That's when I knew exactly where he was. I turned my head and homed in like a missile.

'How do you plead on the charges of grievous bodily harm with intent.'

I felt sick hearing the judge's words of what he'd done to me, and hearing Shane's voice. There was a long pause and then someone behind let out a gasp, then someone else did; the scribbling noise went wild, and people started talking.

'What's happening?' I said in a panic.

'He's just got up and asked to leave,' Lara sneered.

'Without entering a plea?'

'Yes.'

'Can he do that?' I asked, shaking my head in disbelief.

'There's nothing the judge can do if he won't speak,' Lara said.

What a bastard. It had taken all my courage to come to court only for him to leave me hanging.

'I should have known he'd do this to me, I should have known he'd drag out my suffering,' I shouted to my family outside the courtroom.

'He looked so guilty, though, when he saw you, Tine,' Tracey said.

'Good,' I spat.

'He walked in, looked around the court, and then when he saw you his eyes did a double-take.'

'What did he look like?' I had to know.

'He was looking bigger than I'd ever seen him.' Tracey sounded revolted.

'And then what?' I asked.

'He turned his back so he faced as far away from you and us as possible. He had guilty written all over his face. He was really agitated, he kept leaning forward and fiddling with his hands.'

'And then what?' My memories of him were rushing back.

'Then he composed himself. Got up and swaggered out like he thought he was some sort of hero.'

'Bastard,' I seethed, clenching my fists in anger.

The plea hearing had been rescheduled for two weeks' time, which meant I would have to prepare myself all over again. I couldn't relax until I knew whether there would be a trial, whether I would be expected to stand up in court and tell every-one how he'd gouged my eyes out.

I'd got myself so worked up that the comedown was like fall-ing off a mountain. Luckily I was at Danielle's house that evening; she was calm and rational and never judged me. She made me a cup of tea and I hugged it with my hands like it was a hot-water bottle.

'Are you OK?' she asked tentatively. I imagined her frowning.

'No, not really,' I whispered. 'Hearing his voice just brought it all back.' I felt my eyes starting to burn.

'That's normal, you can't be expected to get over it just like that,' Danielle said, and reached for my hand.

'No, no, no, don't let me cry.' I winced as the pain rose up again like a fountain. 'But I still love him,' I admitted, shaking my head.

This time the fountain overflowed and I cried for the first time since the attack.

'Oh my God!' I screamed, clutching my eyes as the salty tears burned my skin. I wanted to stick my head in an ice-cold bucket of water.

Even saying I loved him hurt me.

'You're crying,' Danni gasped. 'Let it out, girl, let it out, have a good cry.' She stroked my back like a baby as I wept.

'How can I think I love him when he's done this to me,' I sniffed. I was so distressed and confused.

'Because you thought it had to be love to justify to yourself why you put up with all his shit,' Danni said as she tried to calm me down.

'He bullied you, beat the shit out of you, brainwashed you into thinking you couldn't do better. You hear his voice for a few seconds today and he's got you under his spell again.'

'No, I won't let it happen,' I said, wiping the tears from my swollen cheeks. 'He's not having me this time.'

'That's my girl,' Danielle said, and hugged me.

I felt like such an idiot when I woke up the next morning, and wished I could take my words back. I apologised to Danni for drivelling on about Shane and swore I was going to get on with my life as she dropped me back at Lorraine's. I perched on my favourite kitchen stool, determined to be strong and not let my blindness get the better of me, but after a couple of hours I just wanted to crawl into a hole and never wake up.

My life had turned into the film *Groundhog Day*. I felt trapped, living the same day over and over, and my living hell was prolonged by Shane refusing to enter a plea again. This time around he never even made it to the court because he wouldn't get in the police van to take him there. Until Shane entered a plea my life was in limbo. I wasn't alive, I wasn't dead, I was somewhere in between.

I hit rock bottom while staying at Paul's house. I'd been there for a few days so I could spend more time with my boys, but I just didn't want to move from the makeshift bed he'd set up for me in the living room. I couldn't stop crying, and I hid my head under the duvet so my kids wouldn't see me.

'Mummy, you've got Terminator eye,' Liam said, referring to the white cap the doctors had inserted in my left eye.

'It's my magic eye,' I told him. I was trying to be playful but what I really wanted to do was die.

For the first time I wished my kids hadn't been in the house that night so Shane would have finished me off. I was wishing terminal illnesses like cancer on myself. I wanted out, I'd had enough.

'I think I need help,' I whispered to Paul as he sat helplessly at the end of my bed. I imagined his tall skinny body stooped over as he ran his hands over his shaved head.

'I need to be sectioned,' I said, and almost choked on my words.

'No you don't, you're just very unhappy,' he said, doing his best to calm me. 'I'll get you an appointment with the doctor first thing. It's going to be OK,' he assured me, but I knew that was a lie. I was buggered.

I saw the GP the next day and he diagnosed me with post-traumatic stress disorder. I was prescribed antidepressants and the GP did all he could to help. For legal reasons counselling wasn't possible because it might affect my statement if Shane's case did go to trial. His refusal to enter a plea was stopping me getting help. Hadn't I paid enough for my mistakes?

Shane still controlled me like a puppet on strings.

23

Waiting Game

'Can I speak to her?' a passer-by asked my sister as she pushed my wheelchair through the high street in Penzance.

It was like people thought I was made of glass and might shatter at any moment.

'I read about what happened to you in the paper,' the middle-aged lady with a strong Cornish accent said.

'Yeah,' I sighed. I wasn't ready for this. I shouldn't have come into town to get my hair done. Lorraine fended her off while I sunk my head in shame.

'Everyone is judging me,' I whimpered. 'I bet everyone thinks what a stupid idiot I am, that I deserved it.'

'No one is judging you,' Lorraine said, and squeezed my shoulder.

But her words fell on deaf ears – I was convinced the world was laughing at me. None of the girls in the salon mentioned Shane or anything about my eyes but it was the elephant in the room. I was paranoid they were all giving each other looks and I couldn't get home fast enough.

Home was now my three-bed house in Penzance. I'd waited four months to move in with my kids and now I was there I could finally relax. Tracey had been appointed my carer by social services and she was there every day, cooking and cleaning up after me while all I wanted to do was sleep. I'd snooze all through the day and then wake up in the middle of the night, binge on some biscuits and then go back to sleep again.

My weight had plummeted to six and a half stone and the skin all over my body had shrivelled so tight that it was painful to walk. I could only stand up for a minute at a time before my legs would shake and I would collapse to the ground. The doctors were worried my heart was going to pack up at any minute and were warning me if I didn't eat I would die.

But I couldn't eat because I had no appetite and I was still throwing up from the trauma of the attack. All I wanted to do was sleep because that's when I dreamed I could still see. I was living when I was sleeping.

My dreams kept taking me back to the same place, when I was five years old walking along the beach with Tracey. The sun's rays were dancing over the waves and I could feel the water lapping between my toes like it was yesterday. Suddenly the sand gave way beneath me and I was being sucked into a hole.

'Help!' I screamed.

The quicksand had eaten my legs and was now as high as my waist.

'Tina!' Tracey shouted, trying to pull me out with her little arms.

'Help, help!' we yelled in chorus as I sank deeper and deeper.

'Tina, wake up.' Tracey shook me from my nightmare. 'The doctor's here to see you,' she said.

'I just want to sleep,' I moaned.

'Come on, Tina,' Tracey encouraged, and nudged me to sit up.

Every day I had people coming around to check on me, the doctor, social services, worried friends. The only person who could help me, though, was Lara, as she would be the one to deliver the news of when Shane would finally make his plea. He'd managed to buy another six weeks of time, claiming he was mentally unfit to decide whether he was guilty or not guilty. I'd worked myself up into a state preparing for the big day only to be told I'd have to go through it all again.

I crawled back into my bed after the doctor had left, wishing I could sleep through the next six weeks. This time I dreamed of Shane. I was walking alone through Penzance high street when I heard girls cackling behind me. I spun around to see Shane with two blondes on either arm, his head rolling back with laughter.

'Look at the state of you,' he sniggered.

I saw my face in the reflection of a shop window and I dropped to my knees. My head was swollen as big as a watermelon, with one eye bulging out like Marge Simpson and a hole where the other one should be. That was how I imagined I looked to everyone.

'No, please God, no!' I woke up screaming.

'Tracey,' I cried out.

'Tracey, do I look really ugly?' I asked as the tears dripped out of my holes.

'No, Tine, you're still beautiful,' she said. 'The swelling has gone down loads.'

'What about my right eye? How does that look?' I badgered.

'It just looks like it's half-closed but you can't really tell,' she tried to reassure me.

But my right eye, which still had the eyeball pushed in, felt like it was drooping. The whole right side of my face felt like it had sagged down like a mud slide. I wasn't ready to take off my sunglasses in public yet.

I slithered under my duvet again. This time I wanted to sleep until my hospital appointment next week when I was due to get my glass eye.

'Tina, why don't you come and watch some TV downstairs for a bit,' Tracey tried.

'I can't follow what anyone's saying. Just leave me, Trace, I'll come down in a minute,' I pleaded.

'You're going to have to face the world one day,' Tracey muttered. I knew she was frustrated with me but I'd had it with the world. I was only here on earth for my kids and as a warning to what can happen if you don't leave a violent relationship.

It was a relief to finally get a glass eye. I'd hated the idea when the old lady in the hospital had said I could get one just like hers. But six months later the thought of not looking like 'Terminator' any more gave me the first bit of joy in a long time.

'So shall I go green this time? Or maybe brown?' I joked with Lorraine as I waited for the doctor to prepare his equipment.

'No, you have to go blue. You've always been a blonde, blue-eyed beach babe,' Lorraine insisted.

'Maybe I could have different colours for different occasions. Is that possible, doctor?'

He laughed as he lifted my chin up to inspect my healing wounds.

'So, what is it to be?' he asked. I could hear him smile.

'Blue,' I decided. 'What does it look like, Lorraine?' I squealed.

'It's so weird, it's like half an eye,' she told me. She sounded fascinated.

'That feels so weird,' I said, squirming as he inserted the cap from the inside corner.

'Wow, Tina, it looks amazing,' Lorraine gasped.

A smile crept across my mouth, the first in months.

Liam was the first to see my new eye and he reached his little hands out to touch my face.

'Mummy, your eye is better,' he chirped.

'Yes, Liam, Mummy is better,' I said, tickling him.

'You can see again, Mummy,' he giggled.

'Yes, I can see you,' I lied. I didn't have the heart to tell him the truth.

I'd been home for less than an hour when disaster struck. I wasn't used to my new eye and forgot I had to be gentle when I wiped it. I felt something pop and my glass eye flew out of my socket and by some miracle landed in my open palm.

'Oh my God,' I shrieked. 'Lorraine, my eye's fallen out, help me.'

'You're joking?' she squealed, hiding behind the door.

I was now on the edge of my seat with my hands cupped, terrified to move an inch in case I lost my eye.

'What are we going to do?' Lorraine asked as she knelt in front of me.

'You saw the doctor put it in,' I said. 'Do you think you could do it yourself?' I was desperate.

'Oh God,' she muttered. I could imagine Lorraine recoiling with horror.

'You can do it, Lorraine,' I urged her.

She made a whining noise as she carefully lifted the eye out of my palm.

'This is gross,' she groaned.

It took several goes but Lorraine managed it in the end. I was really proud of her. She broke down into nervous giggles.

'Come here,' I said, and reached out my arms to hug her. We both shook with laughter at the horror of the moment we'd just shared.

That night I dreamed I could see and I was riding horses like I used to do when I was a teenager. I imagined I had to break in a wild stallion that didn't want to be tamed. I jumped on its bare back, dug my heels in and could feel the wind in my face as if it was really happening.

'Look at me,' I cried out in happiness.

I could smell his mane as I buried my nose into his thick neck – I could feel his coarse hair tangled between my fingers. I jolted awake, still thinking I was in the paddock. I should have known by now it was just a dream but I was still holding on to the hope that some miracle might happen.

The dreams became more vivid and twisted as Shane's court date approached in November. I'd dropped another half a stone in weight and didn't know how I'd be able to make it to court even if I wanted to. I'd wake up at 5 a.m., sometimes earlier, but it would be impossible to get back to sleep so I'd switch on the TV for chat-show programmes like Jerry Springer and Jeremy Kyle. Listening to other people's problems made me feel slightly less sorry for myself.

I was struggling to breathe through exhaustion when Lara told me that Shane had yet again managed to get a stay of execution. He'd asked for more mental assessments and the court date had been rescheduled for the first week in January 2012.

'How is it fair that he's getting all these mental assessments when I'm not allowed any counselling and I'm the one who's lost my bloody eyes?' I gasped. 'How is this right?'

I pleaded with Lara for some reasonable explanation.

'He's being treated like a king in there while I've had everything taken away from me. I'm living in a prison, not him,' I cried. I was on the point of no return.

'Hang in there, Tina,' Lara urged. She wanted me to keep fighting. 'We will get him, he will be prosecuted,' she said.

'But I don't know if I can hang on any longer,' I admitted. The flame inside me was flickering out.

Lara wasn't the only bearer of bad news – Lorraine had discovered where Shane had disappeared to after he'd gouged out my eyes. I wanted to know but didn't want to at the same time, because my first thought was that he was screwing some other girl. He wanted me to think that every time he disappeared.

'Where did you hear it?' I asked Lorraine tentatively.

Lorraine said that a woman she'd never seen before in her life approached her while she was getting a health check at the hospital.

'She asked if I was Tina Nash's sister,' Lorraine started. 'I said yes, hesitantly, because I didn't know who the hell she was, and then the colour drained from her face. She was shaking her head as she told me how she saw Shane the night after he attacked you. I asked her, "What do you mean?" and she said he was at a party with her.'

'A party, I bloody knew it!' I shouted.

'That's not all, Tine,' Lorraine warned me.

'Go on,' I pushed. I had to know now.

'She said Shane was at this party and he was bragging about what he'd done to you.' Lorraine could barely repeat the woman's words.

'Shane told her he had gouged out your eyes, and . . .' Lorraine paused.

'And what? Tell me, Lorraine,' I demanded.

'And your eye made a "pop" noise when it came out,' Lorraine said as she finished the horror story.

I took a moment to hold down my vomit. I froze like a statue with my hands clasped across my stomach and my head down.

'Are you OK, Tine?' Lorraine checked.

'Yeah, I'm still here,' I shrugged.

'So this woman went ballistic at him, telling him he was a sicko. She asked where your kids had been while this was going on and Shane smirked and said they were in bed. Everyone at the party was telling her to shut up because Shane was a psycho, but she wouldn't.'

'What did she say?' I gasped, shocked at anyone who would dare stand up to Shane Jenkin.

'She shouted he was sick and told the room she wouldn't keep quiet,' Lorraine said.

'Did she tell the police?' I asked.

'I dunno.'

'You have to tell Lara, Lorraine.' I was now shaking. 'It might affect the trial, it might help the police to get him to plead.'

'I'll call Lara now,' Lorraine said, and picked up the phone. I listened to the sick story again as Lorraine retold it to the police. I couldn't get my head around how Shane had bragged about popping my eye out. I thought he was in hiding that night, but no, he was bloody partying, getting off on what he'd done to me.

Lara assured us she would look into it and I tried to distract myself in the meantime. I threw the tiny bit of energy I had into making Christmas wonderful for my kids. I felt guilty for what I'd put my boys through, and for not being able to look after them properly any more. I wanted to let Ben and Liam know how much I loved them by splashing out on presents and decorations.

Paul lent me his plastic modern-looking tree for the front room and went on a shopping spree armed with my wish list.

'You're joking, aren't you?' he said as he took notes.

'No, and make sure you get silver tinsel, not gold,' I teased. I'd always known what I liked and didn't like and Christmas was no exception. Last year's celebrations had been a write-off with Shane ripping up his presents, so this year was going to be all about family and the friends who had supported me.

Paul came back later that day with bagfuls and I sat on the sofa and directed him like an orchestra conductor. The mistletoe went on the mantelpiece. The nativity ornaments got scattered over my shelves and table. Paul pinned a 'Merry Christmas' silver banner on my wall and wired twinkling fairy lights through the tree.

'All done,' he said.

I stared into darkness, wishing I could see all his hard work.

'I bet it looks brilliant,' I said, imagining how it might look. 'Thanks, Paul.' I smiled sadly.

My sisters helped me shop for presents for the boys. I knew what I was after and they would drop me outside the store so I could rush in and out without having to chat to anyone. One of my favourite things about Christmas has always been wrapping presents and I was determined to still manage it. While the boys were asleep upstairs I was in the front room rolling out the Christmas paper across the dining table. I cut off dozens of pieces of Sellotape and stuck them around the edge of the table for when I needed them. The first attempt felt like a disaster but pretty soon I'd mastered how to cut the paper to size and make my folds tidy.

'Yes, I can still do this,' I sang, clapping with joy.

I could only manage a couple of presents at a time before I was panting with exhaustion but by Christmas Eve I was tying bows and writing messages on name tags.

Lara got back to me with the news that the witness wasn't the only one – Shane had been at a party bragging about popping my eye out. In fact, he'd been partying for four days according to the people she'd interviewed.

'You would have thought someone would have turned him in,' Lara said.

'No, everyone was scared of him, just like I was,' I explained. I knew first-hand how he could make people shake with fear. 'I bet everyone thought if he'd popped his girlfriend's eye out what the bloody hell will he do to me if I grass him up.' I was trembling from just remembering how he made me feel.

'You're probably right, Tina,' Lara agreed.

Shane was like a maggot in an apple, he was still there, eating me up from the inside. I couldn't get closure until I knew for certain he was going to be locked behind bars forever. I had to try my best to shelve my anxiety, though, because I couldn't let Shane ruin another Christmas.

Paul came over in the morning for present-opening time and I could hear Ben and Liam's expressions as they unwrapped their computer games, clothes and trainers.

'Oh wow, oh wow,' Ben yelped with joy at his new Xbox. 'Thank you, Mum,' he said, and kissed me on the cheek.

'That's all right, Ben,' I told him, tears of happiness welling up.

Paul threw on his chef's hat and cooked us all an amazing turkey roast. It hadn't been much of a Christmas for me but the boys were very happy and I did it for them. I was living for them now – they were all that mattered.

The celebrations took it out of me and all I wanted to do for the next week was sleep until Shane's court appearance after New Year. I started having panic attacks where my chest would feel so tight I couldn't breathe; I'd hyperventilate and the room would spin like it did when Shane used to squeeze all the air out of me. It could take an hour sometimes to calm down and steady my breathing and the attacks could strike at any moment.

I was convinced I was going to die, I was so weak. I didn't even know if I'd make it to court. Shane might not be strangling me now, but he was still taking my last breath.

24

Enough is Enough

'I'm sorry, Tina, we're not going to court.' Lara broke the news.

'What?' I shrieked.

'Shane's still saying he's unfit to plead.'

'No, no,' I cried, and sank my head into my hands.

I'd had sleepless nights, anxiety attacks, nightmares. I'd lost so much weight over this court case my hip bones and ribcage were jutting out.

'It's been rescheduled for April,' she finished.

A missile of pure anger rocketed through me and I rose to my feet.

'I can't fucking believe this!' I shouted, waving my hands in the air. 'I've fucking had enough.'

It was the fourth time he'd pulled out, I'd put my life on hold for nearly a year waiting for him to enter a plea and I'd had it.

'I'm sorry, Tina, I didn't want to tell you this,' Lara tried to console me. 'Coming up here and telling you this was the worst thing I could think of doing.'

Poor Lara had never seen me like this; I never got mad like this.

'Oh God, I don't feel right,' I spluttered as my legs started to shake.

A warm feeling rose inside me like a tidal wave and my heart started to race so hard my breath couldn't keep up with it.

'I can't breathe, I can't breathe,' I said, gasping for air.

'Tina, are you OK?' Lara tried to grab me.

'I need water,' I said, shaking her off and stumbling to my downstairs loo.

I filled the cup I kept by the sink and threw the water over my head. The shock of the cold helped steady my breathing. I hosed myself again and again. Water was splashing everywhere.

'Tina, can I help you?' Lara was by my side.

'No, I'll be fine,' I rasped. I slid down into the puddle and inhaled deep gulps of air until I could speak.

'Do you get these panic attacks a lot?' Lara asked, helping me to my feet.

'All the time,' I mumbled.

Usually I would have been humiliated for Lara to see me in such a bad way but I'd had enough. I didn't care what people thought of me any more.

'I don't want to know any more. I don't want to know until the day he goes to bloody court because I can't do this any more,' I insisted as Lara led me back to my sofa.

'You've been so strong, Tina, don't give up now,' Lara said. She always tried so hard to give me my confidence back.

'You're so kind to me, Lara,' I thanked her.

'Hang in there.'

'I don't want to any more. I've had enough.' I curled my legs into my chest. 'I've had enough.'

Lara was reluctant to leave me but I promised I wasn't going to do anything stupid, I had my kids to think about. I just wanted to be on my own to grieve the loss of all that wasted emotion spent on another court appearance. To grieve the loss of my life.

I went to bed early that night hoping I'd have one of my happy dreams. I liked the ones where I was walking along the beach with my boys and I could see the sand, the sea, the kites high in the cloudless sky, and taste the salty air. I hadn't had one of those in weeks. I pulled the duvet over my face and drifted off to the world I lived in.

I woke up early as usual to a bitter-cold January morning. I imagined my warm breath puffing in front of me as I wrapped my dressing gown over my bony shoulders. I took a moment as something didn't feel right, something had changed.

I had changed.

It felt like a switch had been flicked inside me and I was looking at the world through different eyes.

I can't put my life on hold any more, I need to get on with my life. I'm moving on.

'I need to start living,' I told my empty bedroom.

My family and friends had helped me choose furniture for my house over the four months since I'd moved in, but I still hadn't unpacked any of my clothes or shoes. I was still sleeping among boxes piled high; it was almost a symbol for the fact I hadn't managed to move on from the attack, from Shane.

I wobbled to my feet and patted my hands to the first box I could grab. I peeled off the duct tape with a triumphant tug and dipped my fingers in. I pulled out what I thought was a T-shirt.

'I like that T-shirt.' Ben had crept up on me.

'Oh, morning, Ben,' I croaked.

'Do you want a hand, Mum,' he said, sitting on my bed.

'Yeah, I would, thanks,' I replied, and smiled.

I knew whether I was holding a jumper or a T-shirt, I just needed Ben to tell me what colour it was so I'd be reminded which top it was.

'What colour is this, Ben?' I asked.

'Green.'

'Yep, I know what that is,' I said, threading a hanger through the neck and sliding it into my wardrobe. Whites were on the left, then greys, then reds, greens, and then darks.

I got an incredible rush from taking control of my life and I could tell Ben loved helping me. He'd only been able to make me cups of tea until now but he was always asking if he could do things for me. We were sorting my clothes for a good hour and a half, which was a massive achievement considering I could barely stand.

'Mum, I'll help you make your whole bedroom look nice,' Ben said when my legs finally gave way and I asked him to brew me a tea.

'I'd love that, Ben,' I told him, and a pang of happiness pricked my heart.

I was so exhausted I went to bed early that night but the next day I was back unpacking, this time for two hours. I was determined to make my bedroom smart and tidy. I couldn't wait to show Tracey when she came round on Monday to look after me.

'Oh my God, Tina,' she said as she inspected my colour-coordinated wardrobe. 'Very good, well done,' she said, like she was congratulating a child.

But I was like a kid learning to do things again. Hanging out my clothes were baby steps but it had given me the confidence to do more.

'What brought this on?' Tracey asked.

'I just had a sudden change of heart. As long as Shane is behind bars then I don't care what happens to him,' I said. 'He can rot in bloody hell for all I care. I just thought, eff you, I'm getting on with it.' I lifted my chest proudly.

'That's my girl,' said Tracey. She sounded so proud of me.

'I want to live, Trace, I don't want to be a victim any more.'

It was a struggle, but I started eating more, which gave me energy to fight for my life, and I also stopped throwing up. I got up every morning wanting to push myself to do something new. Tracey laughed her head off when she saw me practising ballerina moves in my hallway.

'I should have been a ballerina,' I joked, pulling my arms up into a pirouette.

'It's good to have the old Tina back,' Tracey giggled.

My biggest fear was going out in public, because I was terrified people were going to stop me in the street and tell me how I'd deserved it. I'd only been out a handful of times but now I was ready to face the world. I started taking my kids to the local pub for Sunday lunch carveries and I went into town for a facial and manicure. Letting a stranger massage my face forced me to let go of my inhibitions. I had to believe I wasn't the monster I'd feared I was, even though my family promised me I wasn't. I started wearing make-up again – foundation and bronzer on my cheeks.

I even managed not to get worked up about Shane's court appearance on Monday 16 April. I hadn't had a panic attack in a while, and I wasn't going to lose sleep over him again. My life was about me now, not Shane.

'Hi, Tina.' Lara's phone call had caught me in the middle of putting the washing on.

He's pulled another bloody sickie, I bet he bloody has.

'Can you be in court tomorrow?' she asked.

'What? Tomorrow as in Friday?' I gasped.

'The CPS have brought the case forward because the press have got wind of it and we don't want a circus in court.'

That gave me less than twenty-four hours to prepare for coming face to face with Shane. I took a deep breath and straightened my back.

'OK, bring it on, I'm ready for it,' I said. 'I don't care any more, Lara, there's nothing more he can do to upset me because he's already done it.'

'Well done, Tina, you're a fighter.' Lara gave me her usual pep talk to gee me up, but then told me she was poorly with the flu and wouldn't be able to be there with me.

'I'll drive you to meet Anna and she'll take you,' she croaked. Lara had once again gone beyond the call of duty to help me and I couldn't thank her enough. It was a blow not to have my pillar of strength there to lean on but I was determined to stay strong. I checked in with my family but it was too last-minute for any of them to come with me. Tracey and Lorraine said they would try and make it but it looked as if I would be facing Shane alone for the first time.

I woke up early on Friday the 13th. I wasn't usually superstitious but I couldn't help thinking it was a bad sign. I crept downstairs and lit a cigarette to steady my nerves.

Shane is so arrogant he's going to plead not guilty, I thought. Why would he keep me hanging on for a year to go guilty? It's not guilty, I know it.

I inhaled deeply.

I knew it was around 7 a.m. by the sound of the cheeping spring birds. Mornings were my special calm time when my eyes were rested so I could think without the pain. I didn't have a clue if Shane would show up but I didn't care any more.

'The show must go on,' I told my living room. I rose to my feet and felt my way back upstairs so I could have a shower, straighten my hair and do my make-up.

Thanks to my colour-coordinating I knew exactly where to find my outfit. I carefully picked out a white top and pink cardigan to go over some fitted blue jeans and I wore my white and pink Nike Air trainers to match. I put on my sunglasses and I was ready to go.

'How are you feeling?' Lara asked when she picked me up.

'Great,' I chirped. 'He can't scare me any more.'

The spell had been broken.

'And thanks for doing this, you've been my rock,' I told Lara, who had now become my trusted friend.

'You're an incredibly brave woman, Tina. Good luck today,' she said, and hugged me.

Anna took over outside Truro Crown Court and held my arm as she led me up to the white building which I remembered looked like a Greek temple with steps and pillars.

'Tina!' I heard my name bellowed across the car park by a deeply spoken man. It was Chief Detective Inspector Chris Strickland.

'Hi, Chris.' He had an air about him that said he was an important guy.

'How are you feeling today?' He sounded concerned.

'Yeah, I'm feeling good. I feel like it's a day out,' I said with a grin.

He started laughing and led the way inside the building. Our footsteps echoed off the high ceilings and I was taken from the throng of police officers into the witness protection room. I was hit with the familiar musty smell of stale air and edged back onto one of the hard chairs.

'Is he here?' I asked Anna.

'Not yet,' she said, and squeezed my arm.

'I bet he doesn't bloody show up again,' I scoffed. 'But I don't care – he can't hide forever,' I said in my second breath.

'Shane Jenkin to Room One, Shane Jenkin to Room One,' the tannoy bleated.

'Oh God,' I whispered. Just hearing his name had made my armour shatter to the ground. I tried to stand up but my legs had turned to jelly. I heard the door open and craned my ear to hear what the police were whispering.

'What? What?' I begged.

'He's here,' Anna said.

'Oh God,' I whimpered. I thought I was stronger than this, I thought I was ready for him.

'Is he in the courtroom?' I asked, my heart pounding.

'No, he'll be let in after you take your seat,' Anna reassured me. 'Are you ready?'

I took a final sip of water to cool my nerves and grabbed her hand. 'Ready as I'll ever be. Let's just hope Friday the 13th doesn't turn out unlucky for me,' I half joked.

Anna took a firm grip on my arm to lead me up the steps.

'As soon as he sees me he's going to start shouting abuse,' I said in a panic. 'He'll call me all those horrible names again, he won't care he's in a courtroom, he's got no respect for the law.'

I slowed down like I wanted to back out.

'As soon as he starts doing that they will march him out the room,' Anna told me, tugging me on.

'But you don't understand, he's a big guy,' I said, and shook my head with frustration.

I edged along the public gallery bench and was sandwiched by cops on either side. Just like that cold morning in January, a switch suddenly tripped inside me and I stopped feeling afraid. I thought I'd be scared not having my family there, but I felt empowered.

'He's going to plead not guilty, I tell you,' I leaned over and whispered to Anna.

There was the usual filing of papers and whispers as the barristers talked among themselves, and then the court fell deathly silent.

Oh God, he's here.

I heard the jangle of handcuffs and footsteps. I faced the other way, I couldn't bear to look at him.

'Is your name Shane Jenkin?' the judge bellowed across the courtroom.

'Yeah,' he acknowledged.

His voice made me feel sick. I still couldn't look in his direction.

'How do you plead? Guilty or not guilty?'

At that moment my head spun around; I couldn't control myself.

Shane took a few seconds and then muttered, 'Guilty.'

Everyone let out a gasp of shock.

I glared at him with hatred and then nodded my head vigorously as if to say, 'Yes, you fucking are.' I then turned to face the other way.

'I can't believe he put me through a year of hell just to say guilty,' I said to myself, and tried to stifle my anger.

'Order,' the judge demanded, trying to silence everyone's surprise at Shane's plea.

'Order,' he repeated, slamming his hammer down.

Shane was led away and I was left reeling.

'I never expected that,' gasped Anna.

'Typical Shane to screw with my head,' I spat. 'I was ready for him to plead not guilty. I wanted to stand up in that courtroom and tell the world what he did to me.'

'He couldn't take his eyes off you,' Anna said.

'I bet he bloody couldn't. I hope he took a long hard look because I'm the reason he'll spend his life behind bars.' I suddenly panicked. 'He will get life, won't he? When will the sentencing be?'

'In four weeks' time. He'll be behind bars for a very long time,' Anna said, in an effort to calm me down.

I could hear the air sail out of me I breathed so deeply with relief.

Lorraine was waiting for me outside the courtroom and she was as speechless as everyone else when I broke the news to her.

'I never thought he'd go guilty,' she said, hugging me. The drama of the day suddenly hit me like a truck and I needed to rest.

'Take me home, Lorraine,' I pleaded.

The relief of it finally being over started to sink in as we drove back to Penzance. I hadn't realised how much energy I'd used preparing for court, but now I could relax. I threw the load I'd been carrying on my shoulders out of the window and nestled back into the car seat.

I felt at peace for the next couple of weeks knowing the end was in sight and I carried on fighting for my rehabilitation. During my special quiet time in the morning I would think about Shane and what he was doing. I'd imagine him sitting on his bed in his cell, staring into space, thinking about how much he wished he'd finished me off that night.

I'd perch on the edge of my sofa with a table in front of me with my cigarette, ashtray and a glass of water. I'd think about all the promises he'd made and broke. I wondered if he wanted to call me? Did he miss me? Was he sorry? Had he loved me too much, so that he didn't know how to control his love?

I'd push any nostalgic thoughts away and congratulate myself on how far I'd come. I used to miss Shane a lot after the attack, which scared me because I'd imagine him not how he really was. All I could think about were the good times, how sweet and loving he could be, how he'd look at me with those puppy-dog eyes like he'd never been loved before, the special little presents he'd buy, how he'd acted like a dad to my kids.

Now all I miss is the Tina before I met him. I still can't work out why it took me so long to walk away, but when you're in that situation it's hard to see a way out.

I was calm as the sentencing approached. I knew it would be a media circus but I was ready to show the world I wasn't going to be a victim. I had kids – I had a life to get on with. I'd cut myself off from the gossip that was spreading around town but some of the more vicious words got leaked back to me.

'Everyone in the pub was talking about how Shane would be out of prison in three years,' Lorraine said. 'I told them they were talking rubbish but they kept going on and on about it, they were making me so mad.' She was getting riled up just remembering it.

'They don't know what they're talking about,' I snapped. That's what I hated about living in a small town, everyone stuck their nose into everyone else's business.

'They know nothing,' I said, standing up in anger.

'Sorry, Tine, I just thought you should know, everyone is saying Shane will get off lightly,' Lorraine said.

'They can think what they bloody like,' I sniffed, putting on my armour.

But just an ounce of doubt was enough to set me off worrying again. Maybe they were right? Maybe he would be out on the streets in a few years – hunting me down again. My thoughts were scaring me. My hands started to tremble uncontrollably as I imagined him coming after me to finish off the job.

I'm a sitting duck now that I'm blind.

I'd have to move, give up everything I know for him.

No, NO! I shook the dark thoughts from my head.

I was now a bundle of nerves as the court sentencing approached.

25

Justice

I woke up on the morning of 10 May 2012 as calm as the sea in Cornwall on a baking summer day. I pushed all my worries about Shane getting off to the back of my head where I now stored all my painful memories. I had a job to do – to stay focused and strong for all my loved ones.

I'd had my hair cut and coloured last week and Lorraine had done my nail extensions the night before. I wanted to look groomed because I knew the world would be watching me, but mostly I wanted to show Shane that he hadn't taken my dignity away.

I chased Ben to get up for school and got Liam ready for his dad, who'd be looking after him while I was in court. I got in the shower and let the water wash away my first nervous jitters. I methodically laid out my clothes on the bed and made the first big decision of my day.

'Black cardigan or white?' I muttered.

'White – this ain't a funeral, this is a celebration,' I scoffed.

I wriggled into my light-blue jeans and threw on a blue strappy top, then finished off the outfit with my crisp white cardigan. I lit a final cigarette for luck, and then put on my sunglasses.

'Ready?' Lorraine asked.

'Ready,' I acknowledged.

Lorraine, Trace, my whole family and friends were going to be there to support me this time. There was a knock at the door but I knew who it was before I answered.

'Hi, Lara,' I greeted her, and gave her a hug. 'You smell nice,' I told her.

'I've brought my bottle of Dior Addict perfume just like you asked,' Lara said, rummaging in her handbag.

'What's going on here?' Lorraine laughed as Lara spritzed me.

'I wanted to smell nice whatever happens,' I said, the cheeky Tina coming out in me.

I didn't say much on the car journey to Truro because I didn't want anything to break my steely composure. Lara ran through what the procedure would be and how to handle the press. Anna, and what felt like the entire Cornish police force, were waiting for me outside the court.

SNAP! SNAP! SNAP!

The noise of press photographers sounded like gunfire. It had started already. Lara and Anna grabbed my hands protectively and became my bodyguards as they led me up the steps.

This time we were taken into a side room where my barrister Andrew McFarlane could run through what was about to happen. He was a well-spoken man who, I imagined, was in his late sixties. He wasn't like the barristers I'd seen on TV; his voice was warm and caring with no airs and graces – I imagined he looked like Father Christmas without the beard, but with a barrister's wig instead.

He said Shane's defence would speak, then he would sum up our case and then the judge would decide Shane's sentence. I jumped at the mention of his name.

'Is he here?' I asked tentatively.

'No,' sighed Mr McFarlane.

'What, why not?' I charged to the edge of my seat.

'His barrister requested he didn't attend because he is too dangerous to be in court. They thought his reaction to the sentencing could put others at risk.'

'Oh my God,' I gasped.

And then my anger rose up and out of my mouth. Shane *was* a very dangerous man, but it wasn't right that he had once again got out of appearing in court.

'This ain't right, he should be here, I want him to be here,' I snapped.

'It's all right, Tina,' Lara said, trying to reassure me.

'No, it's not all right, he did this to me, he needs to face his punishment. I've made it to every court appearance and I can barely walk,' I said, shaking with anger.

I took a few deep breaths and found my composure again.

'But . . .' I paused. 'I said I wouldn't care if he was there or not, so let's get this over with.' I nodded defiantly to Lara to take me in.

She hoisted me to my feet and led me into the courtroom, where the reporters would be waiting to capture my every move.

Lara and I both tripped on the carpet as we made our grand entrance.

'How embarrassing,' I sniggered, as we'd just about stopped each other from falling. I could feel everyone's eyes burning a hole in me as we shuffled over to where the jury usually sits when there is a trial. I slid into the front row and the police locked me in.

'Who's here?' I whispered to Anna.

She gave me a rundown of everyone in the courtroom and it sounded packed to the brim, with press almost sitting on top of each other in the public gallery. She had noticed a woman who had taken a seat next to the judge.

'Who's this?' Lara said to herself.

'Who? What?' My ears pricked up.

'She's a small lady, very proper with her grey-brown hair styled in a set and blow dry. She looks stern,' Lara whispered. 'That's the Sheriff of Cornwall,' she squeaked as she suddenly realised.

'There's a Sheriff of Cornwall? Is she wearing a sheriff's hat?' I giggled.

'Shhhh,' Lara hushed me as the court fell silent for the judge, Christopher Clarke.

'All rise,' a voice boomed across the room.

Lara helped me to my feet and my stomach lurched. This was it, this was finally it. Shane's barrister was first to make his case and he tried to paint Shane as a nice guy who just had a few mental issues. I shook my head in disgust as we were told he wasn't a threat.

'This isn't right,' I muttered.

The barrister went on to describe what happened the night he gouged out my eyes. He said there was a struggle, that Shane accidentally fell on me.

What?

That Shane accidentally gouged my eyes out.

WHAT?

His barrister argued that there was no "intent" there.

'I can't listen to this,' I said, squirming in my seat. 'Take me out, I can't go on.' I began to rise.

'We can leave if you really want, Tina, but I advise you to wait to hear what our barrister says. That's when things will change,' Lara said, squeezing my arm, which I'd wrapped around hers.

I sat back down and craned my ear to hear the prosecutor, the whole time thinking, *He's going to get off, he's going to get off.* I was sure the atmosphere had changed, that there was now doubt in everyone's minds as to whether Shane meant to take out my eyes.

'The judge thinks it's an accident, I know he does,' I panicked.

Lara squeezed my hand.

There was a long tense silence while the judge read over his notes from the morning's proceedings. You could have cut the air with a knife. I focused on my breathing to stop myself getting a panic attack.

'Ahem.' Judge Clarke cleared his throat and I jolted to attention.

He started off by reminding the courtroom what Shane had done to me.

'Jenkin repeatedly held Tina Nash tightly around the neck and, as he continued to strangle her, she lost consciousness and from time to time she hallucinated,' he said matter-of-factly. 'At some point during this attack when she was unconscious, the defendant gouged out her eyes with his fingers or thumbs.'

The words made me wince. I wondered if the reporters had noticed. Had they scribbled that down?

The judge paused as he built up to his finale.

'Shane Jenkin has committed a truly terrible crime of extreme violence. That violence has left Tina Nash permanently blind. She has lost the precious gift of sight.'

Oh God, he's going to get off.

'She will never again be able to see her family or her friends or the beautiful coast and countryside of this county. For the people who can see the world around them it is almost impossible to imagine having one's sight removed by the brutal act of another human being.'

Oh God, he's going to get off.

I gripped Lara and Anna's hands.

'It is almost impossible to imagine the despair and distress Miss Nash must feel at never being able to watch her two sons growing up,' he finished.

He shuffled through his papers and cleared his throat one final time.

'I hereby sentence Shane Jenkin to an indeterminate sentence which he will serve in a mental hospital. He is to serve a minimum of six years in prison,' he announced.

'Yes, yes,' came cheers from the police all around me. But I wasn't cheering, it sounded to me like he'd be on the streets before I knew it.

'What does that mean?' I turned to Lara in panic. 'Is he getting out in six years?'

'No, Tina, it means he's never getting out because he has to prove himself fit in a mental hospital before he serves his time in prison,' she said, sniffing back her tears of joy.

'He's never getting out,' I said, and broke down.

'No, justice has been done,' Lara confirmed, hugging me.

The judge interrupted our celebrations with his final words: 'It will be many, many years before parole is granted. Shane Jenkin is a very dangerous man from whom the public needs to be kept safe.' His words echoed across the courtroom.

'It's over, it's finally over – I can get on with my life,' I told Lara, smiling through my tears.

Lara and Anna held my hands as they led me out of the courtroom and into the media circus that was waiting for me on the steps.

SNAP! SNAP! SNAP! the cameras fired again. I held my head high; I didn't have to hide any more.

'Tina, Tina, Tina,' reporters cried.

Lara had helped me prepare a speech and I stood holding her hand as she read it out to all the reporters who had closed in on me.

'Tina has prepared a statement,' Lara announced. A hushed silence fell among the rabble as she began to read it.

'Shane Jenkin was not mentally ill when he attacked me, he was not drunk or under the influence of drugs. It was a silent, prolonged attack. Shane knows what he did to me that night and he has to live with that for the rest of his life. My life changed forever that night and will never be the same but I am now able to move on, start my treatment and rebuild my life. I feel nothing towards Shane – nothing – because that's a feeling, and I don't want to have any feelings towards him. I'm not going to waste my time. He never existed.'

I nodded, as if I was saying the words myself.

'I have a future and want to provide a future for my kids and be a good mum. I feel like I'm coming to terms with it now, I don't feel as low as I did. I'm definitely getting the old me back.

'I don't think I'm brave, I think I'm surviving . . . you only get one life, so I'm not going to let him ruin it.'

Lara folded the paper. 'That's all,' she concluded.

'Tina, Tina,' reporters screamed, trying to get me to comment. Everyone wanted a piece of me.

Lara and Anna helped me into the car, closing the door on the chaos. I fell back into the car seat and breathed a huge sigh of relief.

'God, I could murder a cup of tea,' I joked. Lara and Anna burst out laughing.

26

Moving on

'What did you do today, love?' Nan asked. I could hear her pour the tea from a height into my mug.

'Thanks, Nan.' I smiled, feeling my way to the slice of coconut cake she had placed in front of me.

'It's funny, Nan, your cake smells even tastier when I can't see it,' I said grinning.

'You need feeding up,' she croaked. I could imagine her giving me a concerned nod as she said it.

'Well, I've got loads more energy inside me, I spent the whole day shopping in Manchester with Paul,' I said and smiled again.

'Is that right?' Nan said. I could hear she was pleased.

'Yep, my energy has gone through the roof. Half a year ago I couldn't stand for longer than a few minutes and now look at me.'

'I bought loads of skinny jeans in every colour, look, Nan,' I said, rummaging around in the bag by my feet. I pulled out a pair and held them up for Nan's inspection.

'What colour are these?' I asked.

'Yellow, dear,' she said.

'I got a green and a red pair too.' I showed her the others. Being a girl, I'd always loved shopping, and I'd found a way to enjoy it again. Paul had taken me to the Trafford centre for the day and we got a nice system working where I would tell him what I was after, he would pick it out, and I would then feel the material to see if I liked it.

Shopping was one of the many things I was discovering my love for again. I'd always taken pride in my appearance and I was determined not to let myself go just because I couldn't see myself. I'd got back into having my regular facials and mani-cures and I'd started wearing lip gloss when I left the house.

'Do you want me to make you and the boys dinner, love?' Nan asked.

'No thanks, Nan, I promised Ben and Liam fish and chips tonight.' I reached across the table to where Nan always rested her hands.

'It's really sweet of you to offer through,' I said giving her hand a squeeze.

'Well, you know, I worry about you,' she said, the mother in her coming out.

'You don't need to worry, I'm learning to cope. You know I never like people to make a fuss,' I said taking another slurp of tea.

I had come on leaps and bounds – a year ago, all I wanted to do was sleep, and now I fill my days doing household chores. I can put the washing machine on, cook meals in the microwave, and I had every takeaway in Penzance saved on my phone. I take pleasure in the little things like having a cup of tea and cake in the afternoon. I get up early so I can have my quiet time watching TV whilst enjoying my first cigarette of the day. My trampoline, which I used to love sunbathing on, has been replaced with garden chairs and there is nothing that fills me with more joy than feeling the sun on my face whilst hearing my boys laugh and play around me.

'That sound like Danni,' I said, craning my head around to the door. I know everyone by their footsteps now.

'Hi, June,' Danni greeted my Nan. She'd come to take me and the boys for fish and chips on the seafront.

'You ready, Tine?' she asked, holding out her arm to guide me.

I could smell the sea and hear the waves lapping as we walked along the promenade. Now that I was blind my sense of smell, hearing and touch was ten times stronger. Liam's little hand was clasped tightly in mine whilst Ben raced ahead to try and beat the Friday queue in the local chippy.

'Hurry up, Mum,' Ben moaned.

'I'm doing my best, Ben. They won't run out of chips,' I teased. I liked how my boys still treated me the same.

'I've got everything to live for,' I said turning to Danni. I'd had such a perfect day. I wasn't naive enough to think my life was going to miraculously change now Shane had been locked away, but I had found a strength I never knew I had. I was no longer a victim, I was a survivor.

As we chatted like old friends I heard someone say my name.

'What was that?' I asked Danni.

'I dunno,' she shrugged.

'Are you Tina Nash?' a woman with a Northern accent said approaching me.

'Yeah,' I answered hesitantly, grabbing Danni's hand for support.

'I saw you on the news,' she said.

'Oh right,' I said to the tourist. Penzance was full of them.

'Sorry to bother you but I had to tell you how brave you are. To survive what you went through and to come out the other end fighting.' She paused to compose herself.

'You're an incredible woman,' she finished.

I felt the tears prickle.

'Thank you,' I smiled, biting my lip to stop myself crying.

'I don't feel brave, I'm just getting on with it,' I said.

As we walked on to the chippy, a wave of happiness washed over me.

I had everything to live for.

Tina would like to thank:

The reason I wanted to publish my story was to help those in violent relationships realise they are not alone and that there is help out there for you. You are not to blame and you do not have to suffer in silence, there is a whole life waiting for you, so set yourself free.

There are some very special people in my life who I would like to thank, as without them, I would not be here today. Firstly I would like to thank my boy's father for raising the alarm.

I would like to thank the staff at Treliske Hospital in Truro who cared for me and making me feel safe and giving me hope.

I couldn't have got myself back on my feet if it wasn't for my family and a special thanks goes to my mum, nan and sisters for looking after me. My best friends – Danni, Sapphire and Wendy, I love you like family.

I would like to thank the police for not giving up on me and trying to keep me safe. Lara and Anna have been my rocks and I would have crumbled a long time ago if it wasn't for them. Thanks also to Sara Firth for always being there.

I couldn't have told my story if it wasn't for my ghost writer Ruth Kelly who put my words onto paper. Thank you for being so easy to talk to and helping me understand what I went through. Thank you Simon & Schuster for publishing my story, and Kerri Sharp, for your support.

If you think you might be in a violent relationship call the 24-hour National Domestic Violence Freephone Helpline, which is run in conjunction with Women's Aid and Refuge – 0808 2000 247.

According to Women's Aid there are signs to help recognise if you are in an abusive relationship. Although every situation is unique, there are common factors that link the experience of an abusive relationship. Acknowledging these factors is an important step in preventing and stopping the abuse. This list can help you to recognise if you, or someone you know, are in an abusive relationship.

- **Destructive criticism:** and verbal abuse: shouting; mocking; accusing; name calling; verbally threatening.
- **Pressure tactics:** sulking; threatening to withhold money, disconnecting the telephone, taking the car away, taking the children away, or reporting you to welfare agencies unless you comply with his demands; threatening or attempting suicide; withholding or pressuring you to use drugs or other substances; lying to your friends and family about you; telling you that you have no choice in any decisions.
- **Disrespect:** persistently putting you down in front of other people; not listening or responding when you talk; interrupting your telephone calls; taking money from your purse without asking; refusing to help with childcare or housework.
- **Breaking trust:** lying to you; withholding information from you; being jealous; having other relationships; breaking promises and shared agreements.

- **Isolation:** monitoring or blocking your telephone calls; telling you where you can and cannot go; preventing you from seeing friends and relatives; shutting you in the house.
- **Harassment:** following you; checking up on you; not allowing you any privacy (for example, opening your mail), repeatedly checking to see who has telephoned you; embarrassing you in public; accompanying you everywhere you go.
- **Threats:** making angry gestures; using physical size to intimidate; shouting you down; destroying your possessions; breaking things; punching walls; wielding a knife or a gun; threatening to kill or harm you and the children; threatening to kill or harm family pets; threats of suicide.
- **Sexual violence:** using force, threats or intimidation to make you perform sexual acts; having sex with you when you don't want it; forcing you to look at pornographic material; forcing you to have sex with other people; any degrading treatment related to your sexuality or to whether you are lesbian, bisexual or heterosexual.
- **Physical violence:** punching; slapping; hitting; biting; pinching; kicking; pulling hair out; pushing; shoving; burning; strangling.
- **Denial:** saying the abuse doesn't happen; saying you caused the abusive behaviour; being publicly gentle and patient; crying and begging for forgiveness; saying it will never happen again.